THE Concise AACR2

FOURTH EDITION

*Based on AACR2
2002 Revision*

2004 Update

Prepared by

MICHAEL GORMAN

Chicago: American Library Association
Ottawa: Canadian Library Association
London: Chartered Institute of Library and Information Professionals

2004

Published 2004 by

AMERICAN LIBRARY ASSOCIATION
50 East Huron Street, Chicago, Illinois 60611
ISBN 0-8389-3548-6

CANADIAN LIBRARY ASSOCIATION
328 Frank Street, Ottawa, Ontario, Canada K2P 0X8
ISBN 0-88802-311-1

Facet Publishing for the
CHARTERED INSTITUTE OF LIBRARY
AND INFORMATION PROFESSIONALS
7 Ridgmount Street, London WC1E 7AE
ISBN 1-85604-540-4

Library of Congress Cataloging-in-Publication Data

Gorman, Michael, 1941-
  The concise AACR2, 2004 revision / prepared by Michael Gorman.
    p.   cm.
  Includes index.
  ISBN 0-8389-3548-6
    1. Anglo-American cataloguing rules. 2. Descriptive cataloging—Rules.
  I. Title: Concise Anglo-American cataloguing rules, 2004 revision.   II. Anglo-
  American cataloguing rules. III. Title.
  Z694.15.A56G67 2004
  025.3'2–dc22   2004016088

Canadian Cataloguing in Publication Data

Gorman, Michael, 1941-
  The concise AACR2 : based on AACR2 2002 revision, 2004 update / prepared
  by Michael Gorman. — 4th ed.
  Includes bibliographical references and index.
  ISBN 0-88802-311-1
    1. Descriptive cataloging—Rules. I. Title. II. Title: Anglo-American
  cataloguing rules.
  Z694.15.A56G67 2004   025.3'2   C2004-905125-3

British Library Cataloguing in Publication Data

A catalogue record for this book is available from the British Library.
ISBN 1-85604-540-4

08 07 06   5 4 3 2

To the memory
of my father
PHILIP DENIS GORMAN
1903–1980
my mother
ALICIA F. GORMAN
1918–1998
and of my friend
HUGH CRAIG ATKINSON
1933–1986

Contents

PART 1
Description

PART 2
Headings, Uniform Titles, and References

Joint Steering Committee for Revision of AACR

Chair

Peter R. Lewis (1974–1980)
Frances Hinton (1981–1983)
Jean Weihs (1984–1989)
Ben R. Tucker (1989–1992)
Pat Oddy (1992–1996)
Ralph Manning (1996–1999)
Ann Huthwaite (1999–2003)
Matthew Beacom (2003–2004)
Sally Strutt (2004–   )

American Library Association

John D. Byrum (1974-1978)
Frances Hinton (1979–1983)
Helen Schmierer (1984-1989)

Janet Swan Hill (1989–1995)
Brian Schottlaender (1995–2001)
Matthew Beacom (2001–   )

Australian Committee on Cataloguing

Jan Fullerton (1981–1983)
Elaine Hall (1984–1989)
Diana Dack (1989–1994)

Ann Huthwaite (1994–2003)
Deirdre Kiorgaard (2003–   )

British Library

Peter R. Lewis (1974–1978)
J. C. Downing (1978–1980)
Joyce Butcher (1981–1985)

John Byford (1986–1989)
Pat Oddy (1989–1996)
Sally Strutt (1996–   )

Canadian Committee on Cataloguing

Jean Lunn (1974–1975)
Edwin Buchinski (1975–1978)
Ronald Hagler (1979–1980)

Jean Weihs (1981–1986)
Ralph Manning (1986–1999)
Margaret Stewart (1999–   )

CILIP: Chartered Institute of Library and Information Professionals

P. K. Escreet (1974–1978)
Peter R. Lewis (1978–1979)
Eric Hunter (1980–1985)
Alan Jeffreys (1986–1989)

Rodney Brunt (1989–1995)
Susan Brown (1996–2002)
Robert Atkinson (2002–   )

Library of Congress

C. Sumner Spalding (1974)   Sarah E. Thomas (1992–1994)
Elizabeth Tate (1974–1976)   Barbara B. Tillett (1994–   )
Ben R. Tucker (1976–1992)

Editors of AACR2

Michael Gorman (1974–1988)   Paul W. Winkler (1974–1988)

Foreword to 1981 Edition

The idea of a concise text of the *Anglo-American Cataloguing Rules* is older than the idea of a second edition of the Rules (*AACR2*) itself. Michael Gorman first began work on what was then thought of as an "abridged edition" of the British Text of AACR 1967 almost two years before the Joint Steering Committee for Revision of AACR (of which I had the privilege to be the first chairperson) was set up to carry out the task of producing *AACR2*.

The principal stimulus to that first project was the need expressed by librarians in third-world countries for a set of basic rules, stated in simple English, that could be used by relatively untrained personnel for relatively small and uncomplicated catalogues; and that would be compatible with a progress to the use of the full *Anglo-American Cataloguing Rules* as staff grew in training and experience and as the catalogues grew in size and complexity. Accordingly, Michael Gorman set to work with a small steering group consisting of Philip K. Escreet and Geoffrey E. Hamilton (both of whom also served later on the Joint Steering Committee for Revision of AACR). Indeed, the project was within sight of completion when he laid it aside to take on a larger task, as one of the two editors of *AACR2*.

One of the main objectives of *AACR2*, attained by its publication in 1978, was to bring together the separate North American and British texts of 1967; and another was to reorganize and express the rules in a simpler and more direct way. So most of the earlier work on the abridgement was nugatory—or, rather, it was used in other ways than originally planned, in *AACR2* itself. However, the Joint Steering Committee soon perceived that the potential was even greater than had previously been estimated for a version of *AACR2* that would meet the needs of the many practitioners and students in our own countries, as well as elsewhere in the world, to whom the full and comprehensive text of *AACR2* tells more than they need to know, or wish to hear, about standards and procedures for catalogue making and the organization of bibliographic records at a particular time in the development of their own libraries, of their own bibliographic services, or of their own studies.

Our main concern was that the quest for simplicity and conciseness in the smaller or less complex library and bibliographic environments should not be impeded by the full text's need to provide in some detail for the whole range of conditions and complexities in the largest or most fully developed libraries and services. We were convinced, too, that the principles and practice set out in *AACR2* were, in general terms, equally valid at both ends of the spectrum of development of library services, and, to change the metaphor, that a clearance of the least familiar trees from the thickly planted wood we call *AACR* would enable everyone who has a need to enter it to see the wood more easily as a whole and to find his or her way through it safely and surely.

These were the aims that led the Joint Steering Committee to seek and obtain approval from its parent bodies, the authors of *AACR2*, for the creation and publication of a concise text, making use of Michael Gorman's dual experience in preparing the earlier abridgement and editing *AACR2*, and of the reconstituted Joint Steering Committee as the authoritative advisory group to ensure the most effective relationship between the concise and the full texts.

These are what the authors now have every confidence and belief has been accomplished in the CONCISE AACR2. It is a high quality working tool of practical value in all kinds of libraries and in many countries, and it embodies the essence of the *Anglo-American Cataloguing Rules* in their most up-to-date form, with all the benefits that signifies in the wide world of national standards and international harmonization.

PETER R. LEWIS
Director General
Bibliographic Services Division
The British Library

Acknowledgements (1981)

Acknowledgements are due, in the first instance, members of the cataloguing rules committee of the Library Association from 1968 onwards. This shorter edition of the *Anglo-American Cataloguing Rules* has been twelve years in the making. In encouraging me to attempt to produce a standard, though abridged, set of rules, the British cataloguing rules committee is responsible for the present publication in ways which its then members may not be aware. More recently, the Joint Steering Committee for Revision of AACR (JSC) has given me complete support and encouragement. In particular, I wish to thank Peter Lewis (the chair of JSC from 1976 to 1980), Ronald Hagler, Fran Hinton, and Ben Tucker for their interest, comments, and unfailingly helpful suggestions. Many members of the American Library Association's Catalog Code Revision Committee and, subsequently, Cataloging Committee—Description and Access, have provided me with advice and information.

The following individuals have helped me with comments, criticism, examples, and suggestions: Liz Bishoff, John Byrum, Karen Lunde Christensen, Neal Edgar, Anne Gorman, Eric Hunter, Arnold Wajenberg, Jean Riddle Weihs. My thanks are due my graduate assistants at the University of Illinois (1978–80), Elvira Chavaria and Anne Reuland. Wendy Darre, who typed the many drafts of these rules with her inimitable competence and dispatch, was of invaluable assistance. I am grateful to Helen Cline (managing editor, ALA) for the expertise, care, and hard work that she brought to the task of editing this work for publication. Last, I wish to recognize my daughters, Emma and Alice, without whose unfailing help and encouragement this whole enterprise would have been completed sooner.

MICHAEL GORMAN

Acknowledgements (1989)

I wish to reiterate my gratitude to all those named in the acknowledgements in the first edition of the CONCISE AACR2. In particular, I am grateful for the continuing help and encouragement of Helen Cline, Ronald Hagler, and Jean Weihs. I would also like to thank my assistants at the University of Illinois (Lisa Boise and Anne Phillips) and my assistant at CSU–Fresno (Janet Bancroft). I wish to express my appreciation to the many teachers of cataloguing that have used the CONCISE AACR2 in their classes, especially to Ellen Koger who passed on many useful comments. My thanks for many things are due to Karen Schmidt. My special thanks go to Ken Bakewell for all the hard work he has put into compiling the excellent indexes to both editions to this book. My daughters, Emma and Alice, are now grown women of whose accomplishments I am excessively proud. They still think that the editors of cataloguing codes are strange, and who am I to say them nay?

M.G.

Acknowledgements (1998)

I wish to reiterate my gratitude to those named in the acknowledgements in the first two editions of the CONCISE AACR2. In particular, the continuing interest and friendship of Ronald Hagler has meant much to me for many years. I would like to thank Marlene Chamberlain of ALA Publishing for her advice and assistance during the process of creating this edition. My assistant at California State University–Fresno—Susan Mangini—has been her usual indispensable self. I would be lost without her tactful but relentless reminders of deadlines. I am grateful to Jean Weihs for compiling the index to this edition.

The love of my daughters—Emma and Alice—is more important to me than I can say, and Emma's son, Louis, is a light in my life.

M.G.

Acknowledgements (2004)

I wish to reiterate my gratitude to those named in the acknowledgements in the first three editions of the CONCISE AACR2. I owe all the people named therein a great debt accumulated over the more than three decades of involvement with the making and interpreting of cataloguing rules, a pursuit that still intrigues and involves me. I have been inspired by the work of the late Seymour Lubetzky (1898–2003) and, in all humility, hope that the CONCISE AACR2 embodies the principles he advocated so successfully. I repeat my thanks to Marlene Chamberlain and add thanks to Mary Huchting, both of ALA Editions. My assistants, Susan Mangini and Bernie Griffith, of the Madden Library, California State University, Fresno, combine to keep me on the straight and narrow path. I owe many things to my wife, Anne Christine Reuland.

I am eternally sustained by the love of my daughters, Emma Celeste Gorman and Alice Clara Singer, and the love I have for my grandchildren, Louis Dexter Gorman (1996–   ), Bess Rosa Gorman (2000–   ), and Leo Benjamin Singer (2004–   ).

General Introduction

This book is intended to convey the essence and basic principles of the second edition of the *Anglo-American cataloguing rules* (*AACR2*) without many of that comprehensive work's rules for out-of-the-way and complex materials. Those rules from the full text that have been retained have been rewritten, simplified, and, usually, supplied with new examples. This rewriting is intended to highlight the rules for commonly encountered library materials and to make them even more accessible. Although the method of presentation is different, the end result of the cataloguing process should be the same whether one is using the full or the concise text. In other words, the CONCISE AACR2 prescribes the same cataloguing practice as the full text, but presents only the more generally applicable aspects of that practice and presents them in different terms. The user of the CONCISE AACR2 is referred to the full text for guidance on problems not covered by the concise text and for fuller explanation of rules contained in the concise text. To assist reference between the two texts, a table is given (appendix III) that relates the rules in the concise text to their equivalents in the full text.

The CONCISE AACR2 is intended for cataloguing students, cataloguers in a number of different situations, and other librarians. Persons working in small libraries, especially "one-person" libraries, will be able to do standard cataloguing without the necessity of learning all the details of structure and content of the full text. Beginning students of cataloguing, especially those who wish to learn about cataloguing but not to be cataloguers, will find the CONCISE AACR2 a good introduction to the national cataloguing standard. Paraprofessionals engaged in copy cataloguing by use of catalogue records supplied by national libraries or members of bibliographic networks will find the CONCISE AACR2 an accessible guide to standard cataloguing practice. Public service librarians who wish to understand new developments in descriptive cataloguing practice will find the CONCISE AACR2 a relatively brief summary of that practice. Last, cataloguers working in a non-English-language environment will be able to use the CONCISE AACR2 as a readily comprehensible summary of AACR2 practice.

In practical application, the CONCISE AACR2 is likely to be most useful in small general libraries, though it can be used for basic cataloguing in large general libraries and for cataloguing in multimedia resource centres and in nonarchival specialist libraries.

The style and spellings used in the CONCISE AACR2 follow those of the full text in that they generally follow the *Chicago manual of style*[1] and Webster's *New international dictionary.*[2] Where Webster's permits a British spelling as an alternative, that spelling is followed. As with the full text, care has been taken in the CONCISE AACR2 to avoid sexist language and sexist implications in the rules and examples.

The order of rules in the CONCISE AACR2 follows the usual and recommended sequence of cataloguing, in that part 1 deals with the description of the item being catalogued and part 2 deals with the establishment of access points (name headings and uniform titles) to be added to those descriptions, and references to be made to those access points. Separate introductions to part 1 and part 2 begin on pages 5 and 60, respectively.

These rules are based on the idea that one main entry is made for each item described and that this is supplemented by added entries. If, in your catalogue, no distinction is made between main and added entries, use rules 21–29 to decide all the access points to be added to a description and ignore the distinction between main access points and other access points.

Distinguish the headings and/or uniform titles added to the description by giving them on separate lines above the description. If any entry begins with a title proper (that is, the first element of the description—see rule 1B), give the description alone *or* repeat the title proper on a line above the description.

---

1. The Chicago manual of style. — 15th ed. — Chicago : London : University of Chicago Press, 2003.

2. Webster's third new international dictionary of the English language, unabridged. — Springfield, Mass. : Merriam-Webster ; Harlow, Essex : Distributed by Longman Group, c1986.

Example of entry with heading:

```
Basbanes, Nicholas A.
  A splendor of letters : the
permanence of books in an impermanent
world. -- New York : HarperCollins, 2003.
-- 444 p.  -- ISBN 0-06-008287-9
```

Example of one style of entry under title proper:

```
  Thayer Birding Software's Birds of
North America. -- Cincinnati : Thayer
Birding Software, 1996. -- 1 computer
optical disc: col., sd. + 1 user's guide
```

The entries in many online catalogues (OPACs) are in a format in which each area of the entry (heading, title area, publication details, etc.) is presented on a different line and is often labeled. However, even in OPACs, areas should be presented in the order given in these rules and with the prescribed internal punctuation.

Example of one style of entry in an OPAC:

```
Author       Jones, Norah, 1979-
Title        Come away with me
Publisher    Los Angeles : Blue Note,
             2002
Description  1 CD
Standard no. 7243-5-32088-2-0
```

Some rules or parts of rules are designated as *optional,* or are introduced by the word *optionally,* or are presented as an *either/or* choice. Decide which option is to be used and in which circumstances. Base your decision on your judgement of what is best for your catalogue and its users. Make a record of such decisions.

Sometimes a cataloguer needs to exercise judgement and decide on an interpretation. The need for these is indicated in the CONCISE AACR2 by words and phrases such as *if appropriate, important,* and *if necessary.* Apply judgements and interpretations consistently within one catalogue, and, when possible, record each exercise of judgement.

Rules on capitalization and a glossary are given as appendices I and II.

The examples used throughout the Concise AACR2 have been chosen to illustrate commonly encountered cases. Examples drawn from a variety of media and from modern English-language items have been preferred. Remember that examples only illustrate the rules and are not intended to expand on the rules unless a rule specifically says so.

PART 1

Description

Introduction

A bibliographic resource (often referred to as an "item") is a manifestation of a work that forms the basis for a bibliographic description. A bibliographic resource can be a book or other printed document; a Website, database, or other electronic resource; a graphic such as a poster or art work; a video or film; a CD or other sound recording; or any other means by which recorded knowledge and information are communicated. This part of the CONCISE AACR2 contains instructions on how to make a description of such a resource that has been acquired by your library or to which your library gives access (as in the case of remote electronic resources). The description is displayed in a catalogue after having been retrieved by the use of one or more access points established for the item according to the instructions in part 2.

The rules are based on those in part I of the full text of *AACR2*. In the CONCISE AACR2 only the usual case is dealt with. For more difficult materials or for out-of-the-way problems, see the full text.

The CONCISE AACR2 deals with all materials in one chapter (as opposed to the analytical structure of part I of *AACR2* in which each type of library material is dealt with separately as far as description is concerned). Thus, for example, all the rules on physical description will be found in rule 5 and its subrules.

In describing library materials according to these rules, a basic principle is that you describe the actual bibliographic resource in the format acquired by your library or to which your library gives access. For example, a manuscript reproduced as a book is described as a book; a book reproduced on microfilm is described as a microfilm; a text that has been digitized is described as an electronic resource. Do not describe what something was; describe what something is.

The generalizing of the descriptive rules in the CONCISE AACR2 has led to the loss of some nuances of the original text. None of these details affects access to the descriptions. For example, the rules on sources of information in this text may lead to a diminished use of square brackets in the entry. This small loss of a few refinements will not affect the user of a catalogue in which CONCISE AACR2 entries are found.

Not all the elements set out for the description of materials will be needed for a particular item or for a particular catalogue. See rule 0E for a specification of the minimum elements needed. In particular, any detail described as *optional* need not necessarily be included in a description. Most notes (see rule 7) are optional; a note should only be made if it is necessary to the understanding or identification of the item being described, *or* if rule 7 indicates that it is required.

Some measurements prescribed in rule 5D are not metric. Use metric measurements in their place if they are more suitable for the material or the country in which the cataloguing is being done.

If you are cataloguing in a non-English-speaking country or region, substitute your language or your language abbreviations for the English terms or abbreviations specified in these rules. However, do not translate data transcribed from the item being catalogued.

The Description of Library Materials

Contents

0. GENERAL RULE

0A. Sources of information

Most bibliographic resources acquired by a library or to which a library gives access belong to one of the following types of publication. For each type the chief source of information is:

TYPE OF MATERIAL	CHIEF SOURCE OF INFORMATION
Books, pamphlets, and other printed texts (including atlases)	Title page
Electronic resources	The resource itself
Graphic materials (pictures, posters, wall charts, etc.)	The item itself
Maps and other cartographic materials (other than atlases)	The item itself
Microforms	Title frame
Motion pictures and video-recordings	The item itself
Printed music	Title page
Sound recordings	
Discs (CDs)	The disc itself and label
Discs (LPs, EPs, etc.)	The disc itself and label (if two, both taken together)
Tapes	The tape itself and its label(s)
Three-dimensional objects (models, dioramas, games, etc.)	The object itself

The chief source for a *serial* is the chief source of the first issue, or in its absence, the earliest available issue.[1] The chief source of information for an *integrating resource* is the current iteration of the resource.

---

1. The chief source for a printed serial with no title page is (in this order):

   a) the title page for part of the serial
   b) the cover
   c) the caption
   d) the masthead
   e) the editorial pages
   f) the colophon
   g) other pages

If the chief source is, in fact, two or more sources, prefer information from the first listed to the others. For example, prefer the tape itself to its label in the case of tapes.

Use information found in the chief source in preference to information found elsewhere. If the necessary information cannot be found in the chief source, take it from:

1) any other source that is part of the bibliographic resource itself

or

2) any other source that accompanies the bibliographic resource and was issued by the publisher or issuer (for example, online documentation, a container, a printed insert).

If all else fails, take the information from any available source (for example, a reference work) *or* compose it yourself.

If you have taken the information from outside the bibliographic resource *or* have composed it yourself, enclose it in square brackets and indicate the source in a note (see rule 7B5).

0B. Several chief sources of information

0B1. Single part. If a unitary bibliographic resource has more than one chief source of information, choose the chief source according to the following rules.

a) Use the chief source of information with the latest date of publication.

b) If one chief source treats the resource as a single item and the other as part of a multipart resource, use the source that corresponds to the way in which the item is being catalogued (for example, use the multipart source if you are describing all the parts in one description).

c) If the resource contains words (written, spoken, or sung) all in one language, use the source in the language of the resource (for example, use an English title page for a book in English).

d) If the resource is in a number of languages, use the source in the language occurring first in the following list: English, the first occurring source in any other language using the roman alphabet, the first occurring source in any other language.

0B2. Multipart resources (for example, books in two or more volumes). If a resource is in a number of separate parts, use the chief source for the first part. If there is no first part, use the chief source that gives the most information. If the information differs in the chief sources of the other parts, and if the difference is important, make a note (see rule 7B5).

0C. The description

The description is divided into the following areas:

> title and statement of responsibility
> edition
> special area (*only for* serials; maps, etc.; music)
> publication, etc.
> physical description
> series
> notes (a repeatable area)
> standard number

0D. Punctuation of the description

Separate the areas listed in rule 0C by using one of the following methods. *Either* introduce each area (except the first) by a full stop, space, dash, space (. —) as set out here:

```
Title and statement of responsibility. --
Edition. -- Special area. -- Publication,
etc. -- Physical description. -- Series.
-- Note. -- Note. -- Standard number
```

or begin a new paragraph for certain areas as set out here:

```
   Title and statement of responsibility.
-- Edition. -- Special area. --
Publication, etc.
   Physical description. -- Series
   Notes
```
> *(each note occupies a separate paragraph, though notes may be combined—see rule 7A1)*
```
   Standard number
```

or if the description is to appear in an online catalogue in which each area is labeled, use only the punctuation that is internal to each area.

Within each area, introduce each element (a part of an area), except the first, by special punctuation as set out at the head of the rules in this part for that area (1A1, 2A1, etc.).

Omit any area or element that does not apply to the item being catalogued. Omit also its introductory punctuation.

Here are examples of simple descriptions (one for a book, one for a sound disc). Each is set out in the ways specified above.

Example 1. First layout

```
The fair garden and the swarm of beasts
: the library and the young adult /
Margaret A. Edwards. -- Rev. and
expanded. -- New York : Hawthorn, c1974.
-- 194 p. ; 22 cm. -- Previous ed. 1969
```

Example 1. Second layout

```
   The fair garden and the swarm of
beasts : the library and the young adult
/ Margaret A. Edwards. -- Rev. and
expanded. -- New York : Hawthorn, c1974
   194 p. ; 22 cm.
   Previous ed. 1969
```

Example 1. Online catalogue

```
Title          The fair garden and the swarm
               of beasts : the library and
               the young adult.
Edition        Rev. and expanded.
Publisher      New York : Hawthorn, c1974.
Description    194 p. ; 22 cm.
Notes          Previous ed. 1969.
```

Example 2. First layout

```
The way I should [sound recording] /
Iris DeMent. -- Burbank, Calif. : Warner
Bros., c1996. -- 1 sound disc : digital,
stereo. ; 4 3/4 in.
```

Example 2. Second layout

```
    The way I should [sound recording] /
Iris DeMent. -- Burbank, Calif. : Warner
Bros., c1996.
    1 sound disc : digital, stereo. ;
4 3/4 in.
```

Example 2. Online catalogue

```
Title          The way I should [sound
               recording] / Iris DeMent.
Publisher      Burbank, Calif. : Warner
               Bros., c1996.
Description    1 sound disc : digital,
               stereo. ; 4 3/4 in.
```

0E. Levels of detail in the description

As a basic minimum, include *at least* the areas and elements (provided that they apply to the bibliographic resource) set out in this illustration:

```
Title proper / first statement of
responsibility2. -- Edition statement. --
Special area for serials, maps, music. --
First named publisher, etc., date. --
Extent of item. -- Required note(s). --
Standard number
```

Include further information as set out in rules 1–8 when appropriate for your catalogue or your library.

---

2. If the person or body named in this statement is recognizably the same as the person or body chosen as the main entry heading (see rules 23–28) and there are no other words or only the word "by" (or its equivalent in another language) in the statement, you may omit the statement.

1. TITLE AND STATEMENT OF RESPONSIBILITY AREA

Contents:

1A. Preliminary rule
1B. Title proper
1C. General material designation
1D. Parallel titles
1E. Other title information
1F. Statements of responsibility
1G. Items without a collective title

1A. Preliminary rule

1A1. Punctuation

Precede the title of a separate part, supplement, or section by a full stop, space (.).

Enclose the general material designation in square brackets ([ ]).

Precede a parallel title by a space, equals sign, space (=).

Precede other title information by a space, colon, space (:).

Precede the first statement of responsibility by a space, diagonal slash, space (/).

Precede each other statement of responsibility by a space, semi-colon, space (;).

1B. Title proper

1B1. Transcribe the title proper exactly as it is found in the chief source of information except that the punctuation and the capitalization found there need not be followed. See appendix I for rules on capitalization.

```
Gone with the wind

The big money

White mansions

McAuslan in the rough and other stories

16 greatest original bluegrass hits

The 4:50 from Paddington

The Fresno bee
```

Britannica online

WordStar

The electronic journal of analytical
philosophy

Index to the Columbia edition of the
works of John Milton

Washingtonpost.com

Supplement to The journal of physics
and chemistry of solids

Son of the black stallion

Map of Middle Earth

Elvis is dead, & I'm not feeling too
good myself

Les amants

However, do not transcribe introductory words that are not intended
to be part of the title.

| | Sleeping Beauty |
| *not* | Disney presents Sleeping Beauty |

| | NASA quest |
| *not* | Welcome to NASA quest |

1B2. If the name of an author, publisher, etc., is an integral part of the
title proper, record it as such. Do not repeat the name in a statement of
responsibility (see rule 1F1).

The Rolling Stones' greatest hits

The most of P.G. Wodehouse

The complete Firbank

Geographia Al road atlas of London

The new Oxford book of English verse

CNN interactive

When hearts are trumps by Tom Hall /
Will H. Bradley
>   (*a poster by Bradley advertising a play by Hall*)

Proceedings of the Annual Workshop on
School Libraries

1B3. If the title proper consists solely of the name of the person or body responsible for the bibliographic resource or work of which it is a manifestation, give that name as the title proper.

Byron
>   (*a book of poems*)

Waylon Jennings
>   (*a sound recording of performances by Jennings*)

Amazon.com
>   (*the online company's Website*)

International Conference on the Law of
the Sea
>   (*proceedings of the conference*)

1B4. If the bibliographic resource being catalogued is a part of a larger bibliographic entity (for example, a volume of a multivolume set, a disc that is part of a set of discs, a serial that is a continuing part of another larger serial)

> *or* is a supplement to another publication

> *and* the title proper consists of the title of the larger publication and an indication of the part or supplement

> *and* the two parts of the title are not linked grammatically,

give the title proper as the title of the larger entity followed by the indication of the part.

Faust. Part 1

Stocks & bonds today. Supplement

The music of the masters. 1850-1889

1B5. If the title proper of a serial includes a date or numbering that varies from issue to issue, omit this date or numbering. Indicate the omission by " ... " unless the date or numbering occurs at the beginning of the title.

> Report on the ... Conference on AIDS and Alternative Medicine
>> (*chief source reads:* Report on the Second Conference on AIDS and Alternative Medicine)

but   Annual report

not   ... annual report
>> (*chief source reads:* 1987 Annual Report)

1B6. If there is no chief source of information (for example, a book without a title page), supply a title proper (in this order of preference) from the rest of the bibliographic resource, from its accompanying material, or from elsewhere (for example, a reference source). If no title can be found anywhere, make up a brief descriptive title yourself. Give a supplied or made-up title in square brackets and make a note (see rule 7B5).

> [Map of Australia]
>
> [Photograph of Kenneth Williams]
>
> [City of Portolina Website]

1B7. If the title appears in two or more languages, use the one that is in the main language of the bibliographic resource as the title proper. If there is more than one main language, use the title that appears first.

1.B8. If the title proper of a multipart resource changes between parts, retain the title proper of the first or earliest part, and give the later title in a note (see also rule 22B).

1B9. If the title proper of a serial changes, make a new description, and give the earlier title in a note (see also rule 22C). Close the earlier description.

1B10. If the title proper of an integrating resource changes, replace the former title proper with the new title proper and give the earlier title in a note (see also rule 22D).

1C. General material designation. *Optional addition*

1C1. General rule. If you want to use a general material designation as an "early warning" to the catalogue user, give a term from the following list immediately following the title proper.[3]

activity card	flash card	picture
art original	game	realia
art reproduction	kit	slide
braille	manuscript	sound recording
cartographic material	microform	technical drawing
chart (*not* a map)	microscope slide	toy
diorama	model	transparency
electronic resource	motion picture	videorecording
filmstrip	music	

```
The San Joaquin Valley [diorama]

RLG diginews [electronic resource]

Exploring the human body [kit]

HealthWorld online [electronic
resource]

The New York times [microform]

Black and blue [sound recording]
```

For material for the blind and visually impaired, add "(braille)", "(large print)", or "(tactile)" to any of the above terms when appropriate.

```
The banks of green willow [music
(braille)]

Camden [map (large print)]
```

1C2. If the bibliographic resource is a reproduction in another form (for example, a book in microform; a map on a slide; an online encyclopedia), give the general material designation appropriate to the reproduction (for example, in the case of a map on a slide, give "[slide]").

---

3. This list reflects North American and Australian practice as set out in *AACR2*, rule 1.1C.

1C3. Because they are *optional,* general material designations are not given in the rest of the examples in this part (except as needed to illustrate another issue). Do not take this as implying that they should or should not be used in a particular case.

1D. Parallel titles

If the title appears in the chief source of information in two or more languages, choose one of these as the title proper (see rule 1B7). Give one other title (the one appearing first or the one following the title proper) as the parallel title.

```
        Dansk-Engelske ordbog = Danish-English
 dictionary

        Road map of France = Carte routière de
la France
```

1E. Other title information

1E1. Transcribe other title information (for example, a subtitle) appearing in the chief source of information.

```
        Bits of paradise : twenty-one
uncollected stories

        Aspects of Alice : Lewis Carroll's
dreamchild as seen through the critics'
looking-glasses, 1865-1971

        Annie Hall : a nervous romance

        The gate : the Bay Area's home page

        The devil's dictionary : a selection of
the bitter definitions of Ambrose Bierce
```

1E2. If there is more than one subtitle (or unit of other title information) appearing in the chief source of information, give them in the order in which they appear there.

```
        Clawhammer banjo : the return of the
clawhammer banjo : twenty Irish, English,
and American tunes
```

1E3. If the other title information is lengthy and does not contain important information, omit it.

1E4. If the title proper needs explanation, make a brief addition as other title information.

```
Shelley : [selections]

Conference on Aesthetic Values and the
Ideal : [proceedings]
```

1F. Statements of responsibility

1F1. First statement of responsibility. Always give the statement of responsibility that appears first in the chief source of information, unless the name of the author, publisher, etc., has already appeared as part of the title (see rule 1B2) or other title information.

```
Hangover Square / by Patrick Hamilton

Cruising / Jonathan Raban

Honky tonk heroes / Waylon Jennings

Shoot low, lads, they're ridin'
Shetland ponies / Lewis Grizzard

Proceedings / International Conference
on Nematodes

The monocled mutineer / William Allison
and John Fairley

American literature : a representative
anthology of American writing from
colonial times to the present / selected
and introduced by Geoffrey Moore

Amazing universe CD-ROM / produced by
Hopkins Technology
```

but   `The portable Oscar Wilde`
not   `The portable Oscar Wilde / Oscar Wilde`

> *but*   Lady Windermere's fan : the film of
>   the Old Vic's presentation of Oscar
>   Wilde's play
> *not*   Lady Windermere's fan : the film of
>   the Old Vic's presentation of Oscar
>   Wilde's play / Oscar Wilde

1F2. Other statements of responsibility. Give other statements of responsibility that appear in the chief source of information in the form and order in which they appear there. If the order is ambiguous, give them in the order that makes the most sense.

> Snow White and the seven dwarfs : a
> tale from the Brothers Grimm / translated
> by Randall Jarrell ; pictures by Nancy
> Ekholm Burkert

> A saint in America : John Neumann /
> Raymond C. Kammerer and Carl R.
> Steinbecker ; made by Creative Sights &
> Sounds

> Plats du jour / Patience Gray and
> Primrose Boyd ; illustrated by David
> Gentleman

> Xmag : screen magnification program /
> written by Danny Shapiro ; ported to
> Motif by Philip Schneider

> Dougal and the blue cat : original
> soundtrack of the Nat Cohen-EMI film /
> original story written and directed by
> Serge Danot ; English version by Eric
> Thompson ; music by Joss Baselli

1F3. Give the statements of responsibility after the title information even if they appear before the title in the chief source of information.

> Only the lonely / Roy Orbison
> (*disc label reads:* ROY ORBISON
> Only The Lonely)

1F4. If no statement of responsibility appears in the chief source of information, do not supply one. If such a statement is necessary to make the description complete, give it in a note (see rule 7B6).

1F5. If a single statement of responsibility names more than three persons or bodies, omit all but the first named. Indicate the omission by " . . . " and add "et al." in square brackets.

> London consequences : a novel /
> edited by Margaret Drabble and B.S.
> Johnson ; the work also of Paul
> Ableman ... [et al.]
> *(second statement names fifteen other persons)*

1F6. Omit statements of responsibility relating to persons or bodies with minor responsibility for the item. Such minor responsibility includes:

> writing an introduction to a book
>
> performing in a motion picture (see also rule 7B6)
>
> playing a subsidiary role in producing a motion picture (for example, assistant director, make-up artist, editor)
>
> being responsible for the physical production of the item.

1F7. Omit titles, qualifications, etc., attached to personal names in statements of responsibility unless omitting them makes the statement unintelligible or misleading.

> The larks of Surinam / by Robert
> Antrobus
> *(name appears as:* Dr. Robert Antrobus)
>
> Koalas : our friends from Down Under /
> by S.K. Arline
> *(name appears as:* S.K. Arline, F.R.N.Z.S.)

but

> The prisoner of Chillon / Lord Byron
>
> Fruitful and responsible love / Pope
> John Paul II
>
> Horton hears a Who! / by Dr. Seuss

1F8. Add a word or phrase to the statement of responsibility only if it is necessary to make the statement clear.

> ```
> Denmark : a film / [produced and
> directed by] Eigil Kongsted
> ```
>
> ```
> The best man / Tomi Ungerer ; [designed
> by] Bob Cox
> ```
>
> ```
> Strikeout and other simulation games /
> [collected by] Jim Good
> ```

but

> ```
> Red headed stranger / Willie Nelson
> ```
>
> ```
> Catalogue / Liverpool Public Library
> ```

1G. Items without a collective title

1G1. With predominant part. If a bibliographic resource contains two or more separately titled parts and lacks a collective title, make a single description if one of the parts is predominant. Use the title of that part as the title proper and name the other parts in a note. When appropriate, make added entries for the other parts.

> ```
> Cello concerto in E minor, op. 85 /
> Elgar
> ```
> *Note:* ```In the south: concert overture,
> op. 50 and Elegy for strings, op. 58
> also on CD
> ```

1G2. Without predominant part. If no one part predominates:

> *either* make a separate entry for each part (see also rule 7B16)
>
> *or* give all the titles in the order in which they appear in the chief source and make added entries for all the parts other than the first named as instructed in rule 29B8.

If you are making one entry for the bibliographic resource and all the parts are manifestations of works by the same person(s) or body (bodies), separate the titles by a space, semicolon, space (;).

> ```
> The Brandenburg concertos no. 2 &
> no. 6 ; The clavier concerto in D minor
> / Bach
> ```

```
Grand Teton ; Yellowstone National Park
(maps on same sheet)

A survey of spending on foreign
language teaching ; Foreign language
teaching resources / principal
investigator J.L. Pianko
```

If you are making one entry for the bibliographic resource and the parts are manifestations of works by different persons or bodies, give the titles and statements of responsibility in the order in which they appear in the chief source. Separate the titles and statements of responsibility of one part from those of another by a full stop followed by two spaces (.   ).

```
Rosaceae : twelve hand-coloured
etchings / by Fenella Wingift.  Liliaceae
: twelve hand-coloured etchings / by
Pandora Braithwaite
```

2. EDITION AREA

Contents:
    2A. Preliminary rule
    2B. Edition statement
    2C. Statements of responsibility relating to the edition

2A. Preliminary rule

2A1. Punctuation

Precede this area by a full stop, space, dash, space (. —).
Precede a statement of responsibility following an edition statement by a space, diagonal slash, space (/).

2A2. Take information for this area from the chief source of information (see rule 0A) or from any formal statement made by the publisher or issuer either in the bibliographic resource or in material that accompanies it (for example, a container, a record sleeve, online documentation).
Enclose information taken from anywhere else in square brackets.

2B. Edition statement

Give the edition statement as found except:

1) replace words with standard abbreviations
and
2) replace words with numbers where appropriate.

```
New ed.
```
   (*appears in item as:* New Edition)

```
Rev. ed.
```
   (*appears in item as:* Revised edition)

```
Version 3.8
```

```
3rd ed.
```
   (*appears in item as:* Third edition)

```
Windows 95 ed.
```
   (*appears in item as:* Windows 95 edition)

```
TryoPoly. -- Chicago ed.
```
   (*a game with different versions for different cities*)

```
The international herald-tribune. --
Airmail ed.
```

2C. Statements of responsibility relating to the edition

2C1. If a statement of responsibility relates to one or some editions but not to all, give it after the edition statement if there is one. Follow the rules in 1F.

```
A dictionary of modern English usage /
by H.W. Fowler. -- 2nd ed. / revised by
Ernest Gowers
```

```
Anglo-American cataloguing rules. --
2nd ed. / prepared by the American
Library Association ... [et al.] ; edited
by Michael Gorman and Paul W. Winkler
```

```
Version 2.4, corr. / with diagrams by
Harry Weeks
```

2C2. If there is no edition statement, give such a statement of responsibility in the title and statement of responsibility area.

```
Little Dorrit / Charles Dickens ;
edited by John Holloway

From Atlanta to the sea / William T.
Sherman ; edited with an introduction by
B.H. Liddell Hart
```

2C3. If there is doubt about whether a statement of responsibility applies to all editions or only to some, give it in the title and statement of responsibility area.

3. SPECIAL AREA FOR SERIALS, MAPS AND OTHER CARTOGRAPHIC MATERIALS, AND MUSIC

3A. Serials (in all formats)

3A1. Punctuation

Precede this area by a full stop, space, dash, space (. —).

Follow the designation and/or date of the first issue by a hyphen.

Enclose a date following the designation of the first issue in parentheses (( )).

Precede a new series of numbering, etc., by a space, semicolon, space (;).

3A2. Designation of first issue. Give the designation (volume, part, numbering, etc.) of the first issue of a serial. Replace words with standard abbreviations. Replace words with numbers where appropriate.

```
Inside sports. -- Vol. 1, no. 1-

Private eye. -- No. 1-
```

3A3. Date. If the first issue of a serial is designated only by a date, give that date. Replace words with standard abbreviations. Replace words with numbers where appropriate.

```
Master's theses in education. --
1951-
```

If the first issue is identified by both numbering, etc., and a date, give the numbering, etc., before the date.

```
ALCTS network news. -- Vol. 1, no. 1
(May 13, 1991)-
```

3A4. No designation. If the first issue lacks a designation or date, give "[No. 1]-   ". If, however, later issues adopt a numbering, follow that.

```
[Pt. 1]-
```
(later issues numbered: Part 2, Part 3, *etc.)*

3A5. Ceased serials. If the serial has ceased publication, give the designation and/or date of the first issue or part followed by the designation and/or date of the last issue.

```
Quarter horse newsletter. -- No. 1 (May
1973)-no. 17 (Sept. 1974)
```

3A6. Successive designations. If a serial starts a new system of designation without changing its title, give the designation of the first and last issues under the old system, followed by the designation of the first issue under the new system.

```
Language/art/language. -- Vol. 1, no.
1-vol. 3, no. 7; no. 32-
```

3A7. More than one system of designation. If a serial has more than one separate system of designation, give each in the order in which it appears in the chief source of information. Separate the designations by an equals sign, space (=) *or*, if the serial has ceased, by a space, equals sign, space (=).

```
English review. -- Vol. 1, no. 1-= no.
11-
```

```
Syrian studies. -- Vol. 1, no. 1-vol.
5, no. 3 = Issue 1-issue 19
```

3A8. New serial. If the title proper of a serial changes (see rule 22C), make a new description and close the old description (see rule 3A5).

3B. Maps and other cartographic materials

3B1. Punctuation

Precede this area by a full stop, space, dash, space (. —).
Precede a projection statement by a space, semicolon, space (;).

3B2. Scale. Give the scale of a cartographic resource if it is found on the resource or if it can be determined easily (for example, from a bar graph). Give the scale as a representative fraction.[4]
Precede the scale by "Scale".

```
Scale 1:500,000

Scale 1:63,360
```
(*appears on item as:* One inch to a mile)

If the scale appears as a representative fraction and in words, give the representative fraction only.

```
Scale 1:253,440
```
(*also appears as:* One inch to four miles)

If the scale does not appear on the cartographic resource and cannot easily be determined, do not give a scale statement.

If the description is of a multipart cartographic resource with two or more scales that are given, give the statement *Scales differ.*

3B3. Projection. Give the statement of projection if it is found on the cartographic resource. Replace words with standard abbreviations.

```
; transverse Mercator proj.
```
(*scale given*)

```
Transverse Mercator proj.
```
(*scale not given*)

---

4.   1/2 in. to a mile = 1:126,720   2 in. to a mile = 1:31,680
      1 in. to a mile = 1:63,360   4 in. to a mile = 1:15,840
If the scale is given in centimetres (cm.) to kilometres (km.), multiply the km. by 100,000. For example, 1 cm. to 2.5 km. equals 1:250,000 as a representative fraction.

3C. Music (Scores, etc.)

3C1. Punctuation

Precede this area by a full stop, space, dash, space (. —).

3C2. Musical presentation statement. If a statement indicating the physical presentation of the music appears separately in the chief source of information, give it here. Typical musical presentation statements include "Miniature score", "Playing score", and "Full score".

```
Symphony in B flat for concert band /
Hindemith. -- Miniature score
```

4. PUBLICATION, DISTRIBUTION, ETC., AREA

Contents:
- 4A.   Preliminary rule
- 4B.   General rule
- 4C.   Place of publication, distribution, etc.
- 4D.   Name of publisher, distributor, etc.
- 4E.   Date of publication, distribution, etc.

4A. Preliminary rule

4A1. Punctuation

Precede this area by a full stop, space, dash, space (. —).
Precede a second place of publication, etc., by a space, semicolon, space (;).
Precede the name of a publisher, etc., by a space, colon, space (:).
Precede the date of publication, etc., by a comma, space (,).

4A2. Take information for this area from the chief source of information (see rule 0A) or from any formal statement made by the publisher or issuer either on the bibliographic resource or in material accompanying the resource (for example, container, record sleeve, accompanying documentation). Enclose information taken from anywhere else in square brackets.

4B. General rule

4B1. In this area, give information relating to the publisher, distributor, etc., and the date of its publication, distribution, etc.

4B2. If a bibliographic resource has two or more places of publication, distribution, etc., *and/or* two or more publishers, distributors, etc., give the first named place and publisher, distributor, etc. If another place and publisher, distributor, etc., is more prominent in the chief source of information, also give that place and publisher, distributor, etc.

If a place and/or publisher, distributor, etc., in your country is named in a secondary position, *optionally* add that place and publisher, distributor, etc.

> Oxford ; New York : Oxford University Press
> (*if you are cataloguing in the United States*)

> New York : Dutton ; Toronto : Clarke, Irwin
> (*if you are cataloguing in Canada*)

> Burbank, Calif. : Warner Bros. ;
> London: Butterfly Records
> (*if you are cataloguing in the United Kingdom*)

4C. Place of publication, distribution, etc.

4C1. Give the place of publication as it appears.

> London

> Los Angeles

> Tolworth, England

Supply the name of a country, state, province, etc., if it does not appear but is necessary to identify the place.

> London [Ont.]

4C2. If a publisher, distributor, etc., has offices in more than one place, always give the first named place. *Optionally,* give any other place that is in your country. Omit all other places.

> New York ; London
> (*if you are cataloguing in the United Kingdom*)

```
London ; Melbourne
   (if you are cataloguing in Australia)

London ; New York
   (if you are cataloguing in the United States)
```

4C3. If the place of publication, distribution, etc., is uncertain or unknown, leave out this element.

4D. Name of publisher, distributor, etc.

4D1. Give the name of the publisher, distributor, etc., in the shortest form in which it can be understood and identified. Omit accompanying wording that implies the publishing function.

```
        London : MacGibbon & Kee

        Berkeley : Kicking Mule Records

        Rochester, N.Y. : Modern Learning Aids

        London : Cape
   not  London : Jonathan Cape

        London : Allen & Unwin
   not  London : Published by Allen & Unwin

   but  London : W.H. Allen
   not  London : Allen
           (avoids confusion with other publishers called Allen)
```

4D2. If the name of the publisher, etc., is unknown, leave out this element.

4D3. If the person or body named here is a distributor, *optionally* add "distributor" in square brackets.

```
        San Diego Interactive Data Corporation
        [distributor]
```

4E. Date of publication, distribution, etc.

4E1. Resources other than serials, integrating resources, and multi-part resources. Give the year of publication, distribution, etc., of the edition named in the edition area (see rule 2B). Ignore dates of later issues of the same edition. If there is no edition statement, give the year of first publication of the item you are describing. Give the year in arabic numbers.

```
Ottawa : Canadian Library Association,
1985
```

4E2. Serials, integrating resources, and multipart resources. Give the beginning date of a serial, integrating resource, or multipart resource that is not yet completed. Follow the date by a hyphen.

```
1999-
```

Give the beginning and ending dates of a serial, integrating resource, or multipart resource that is completed.

```
2000-2003
```

If the beginning and ending dates of a serial, integrating resource, or multipart resource are not known, omit them and, *optionally,* make a note (see 7B8).

4E3. If no date of publication is found on the item, give (in this order of preference):

a) the year of publication found on material accompanying the bibliographic resource

```
London : Virgin, 1998
```
(found on CD container)

b) the latest copyright year found on the bibliographic resource, preceded by "c" or, for some sound recordings, "p"

```
New York : Knopf, c1954
```

```
New York : Polydor, p1979
```

c) an approximate year preceded by "ca." and enclosed in square brackets.

```
Toronto : Scaramouche, [ca. 1950]
```
(no date found but probably around 1950)

5. PHYSICAL DESCRIPTION AREA

Contents:

5A. Preliminary rule

5A1. Punctuation

Precede this area by a full stop, space, dash, space (. —) or start a new paragraph (see rule 0D).

Precede the other details (i.e., other than extent or dimensions) by a space, colon, space (:).

Precede the dimensions by a space, semicolon, space (;).

Precede the statement of accompanying materials by a space, plus sign, space (+).

5A2. Source of information. Take information for this area from any source, but prefer information taken from the item itself.

5B. Extent

5B1. Bibliographic resources other than books and atlases. Record the number of parts of a resource by giving the number of pieces, etc., in arabic numbers and the name of the resource or parts taken from the following list.

a) *Art pictures.* Use "art original", "art print", or "art reproduction", as appropriate.

```
3 art prints

1 art reproduction
```

b) *Charts, etc.* Use "chart", "poster", "flip chart", or "wall chart", as appropriate.

```
3 charts

2 posters
```

c) *Electronic resources.* If you are cataloguing an electronic resource that is only available remotely, leave this element blank.

   If you are cataloguing an electronic resource that is available locally in a physical carrier, give the number of physical units and one of the following terms, as appropriate:

> computer chip cartridge
> computer disk
> computer optical disc
> computer tape cartridge
> computer tape cassette
> computer tape reel

```
1 computer disk

2 computer optical discs

1 computer chip cartridge
```

Optionally, use a term in common usage to name the specific format.

```
1 CD-ROM

2 DVDs
```

d) *Filmstrips and filmslips.* Use "filmstrip" or "filmslip", as appropriate.

```
1 filmstrip
```

e) *Maps, globes.* Use "map" or "globe", as appropriate.

```
3 maps

1 globe
```

f) *Microforms.* Use "microfiche", "microfiche cassette", or "microfilm", as appropriate. Add "cartridge", "cassette", or "reel", as appropriate, to "microfilm".

```
7 microfiches

1 microfilm reel
```

Optionally, if you have used the general material designation "microform", omit "micro" from the statement of extent.

```
7 fiches

1 film reel
```

g) *Motion pictures.* Use "film cartridge", "film cassette", "film loop", or "film reel", as appropriate.

```
4 film reels
```

Optionally, if you have used the general material designation "motion picture", omit "film" from the statement of extent.

```
4 reels
```

h) *Music.* Use "score" and/or "part", as appropriate.

```
1 score

2 parts

1 score + 12 parts
```

i) *Slides.* Use "slide".

```
3 slides
```

j) *Sound recordings.* Use "sound cartridge", "sound cassette", "sound disc", or "sound tape reel", as appropriate.

```
2 sound cassettes
```

Optionally, if you have used the general material designation "sound recording", omit "sound" from the statement of extent.

```
2 cassettes
```

k) *Three-dimensional objects.* Use an appropriate term (for example, "diorama", "game", "model", "toy").

```
1 diorama

2 jigsaw puzzles

1 paperweight
```

l) *Videorecordings.* Use "videocartridge", "videocassette", "videodisc", or "videoreel", as appropriate.

> 1 videodisc

Optionally, if you have used the general material designation "videorecording", omit "video" from the statement of extent.

> 1 disc

m) *Graphic materials other than those specified above.* Use an appropriate term (for example, "flash card", "photograph").

> 3 photographs
>
> 1 technical drawing
>
> 1 activity card
>
> 2 pictures

If the bibliographic resource has a playing time that is stated on it or its container *or* that can be ascertained easily, add the playing time in parentheses.

> 1 sound disc (35 min.)
>
> 2 videoreels (88 min.)
>
> 8 film reels (105 min.)
>
> 5 sound cassettes (30 min. each)

5B2. Extent of books, atlases, and other printed items. Single volumes. Record the number of pages in the main numbered sequence.

> 327 p.

If there is more than one main numbered sequence, give the number of pages in each sequence in the order in which the sequences appear in the item.

> 320, 200 p.

Ignore unnumbered sequences and minor sequences.

> 327 p.   *not*   [32], 327 p.

```
119 p.      not     xii, 119 p.

300 p.      not     12, 300 p.
```

If there are no numbered sequences or a great many numbered sequences, give "1 v.".

5B3. Extent of books, atlases, and other printed resources (including completed printed serials). More than one volume. Record the number of volumes in a multivolume book or in a "dead"[5] printed serial.

```
3 v.

200 v.

19 v.
```

5B4. Incomplete resources. If a multipart bibliographic resource is incomplete or if it is a "live"[6] serial, give one of the terms listed in 5B1 or "v." (for printed materials).

```
maps

film reels

v.
```

5C. Other details

Give other details as set out here.

1) *Books, pamphlets and other printed text; microforms; music; printed serials.* If the bibliographic resource contains illustrations, give "ill.". If the illustrations are numbered sequentially, give the number in arabic numerals.

```
320 p. : ill.

320 p. : 37 ill.

1 score : ill.

3 microfiches : ill.
```

---

5. A serial that has ceased publication.
6. A serial that is still being issued.

If all the illustrations are coloured, give "col. ill.". If some of the illustrations are coloured, give "ill. (some col.)".

```
320 p. : col. ill.

320 p. : ill. (some col.)
```

2) *Electronic resources.* If you are cataloguing an electronic resource that is only available remotely, leave this element blank.

If a local electronic resource is stated to produce sound or is known to produce sound, give "sd.".

```
1 computer optical disc : sd.
```

If a local electronic resource displays in two or more colours or is known to produce two or more colours, give "col.".

```
1 computer optical disc : col.
```

3) *Graphic resources (two-dimensional).* If the resource is coloured, give "col.".

```
3 filmstrips : col.

7 posters : col.
```

If a filmstrip or slide set has integral sound, give "sd.".

```
3 filmstrips : col., sd.

48 slides : col., sd.
```

If, however, a sound recording merely accompanies the filmstrip or slide set, treat it as accompanying material (see rule 5E) or, if appropriate, as part of a kit (see rule 10C).

4) *Maps, globes.* If the map or globe is coloured, give "col.".

```
1 globe : col.

3 maps : col.
```

5) *Motion pictures and videorecordings.* Indicate whether the motion picture or videorecording is sound or silent by giving "sd." or "si.".

```
1 videocassette (74 min.) : sd.
```

```
1 film reel (30 min.) : si.
```

If the motion picture or videorecording is in colour give "col.".

```
14 film reels : sd., col.
```

6) *Sound recordings.* For analog discs, give "analog" and the playing speed in revolutions per minute (rpm).

```
2 sound discs : analog, 33 1/3 rpm
```

For all other sound recordings, give "analog" or "digital",[7] as appropriate.

```
2 sound discs : digital
```

```
2 sound cassettes : analog
```

For all sound recordings, give the number of sound channels if the information is readily available. Use one of the following terms.

   mono. (*for monaural recordings*)
   stereo. (*for stereophonic recordings*)
   quad. (*for quadraphonic recordings*)

```
2 sound cassettes : analog, stereo.
```

```
1 sound disc (30 min.) : analog,
33 1/3 rpm, stereo.
```

```
1 sound disc (70 min.) : digital,
stereo.
```

7) *Three-dimensional objects.* Give the material(s) of which the object is made, unless the materials are numerous or unknown.

```
2 paperweights : glass
```

```
1 diorama : papier mâché
```

```
1 game : wood & plastic
```

```
1 toy : wool & cotton
```

---

7. A digital recording is one in which the sound is digitally encoded on the item (for example, a "compact disc").

If the object is black and white, give "b&w". If the object is in one or two colours, give the name(s) of the colour(s). If it is in three or more colours, give "col.".

```
1 box : wood & metal, b&w

1 vase : porcelain, blue & white

1 paperweight : glass, col.
```

5D. Dimensions

Give the dimensions of the bibliographic resource as set out here.

1) *Books, pamphlets, and other printed texts; music; printed serials.* Give the outside height in centimetres (cm.) to the next centimetre up.

```
325 p. : ill. ; 27 cm.

3 v. : col. ill. ; 25 cm.

1 score ; 24 cm.
```

2) *Filmstrips and filmslips.* Give the gauge (width) in millimetres (mm.).

```
1 filmstrip : col. ; 35 mm.
```

3) *Globes.* Give the diameter of the globe in centimetres.

```
1 globe : col. ; 12 cm. in diam.
```

4) *Maps and two-dimensional graphic items (except filmstrips, filmslips, and slides).* Give the height and width in centimetres to the next centimetre up.

```
1 map : col. ; 25 × 35 cm.

1 poster : col. ; 30 × 38 cm.
```

5) *Microfiches.* Give the height and width in centimetres to the next centimetre up, unless they are the standard dimensions (10.5 cm. × 14.8 cm.). In the latter case, do not give the dimensions.

```
3 microfiches ; 12 × 17 cm.
```

6) *Motion pictures and microfilm reels.* Give the gauge (width) in millimetres.

```
1 film reel (12 min.) : sd. ; 16 mm.

1 microfilm reel ; 16 mm.
```

7) *Slides.* Do not give the dimensions if they are 5 × 5 cm.

8) *Sound discs and electronic discs/disks.* Give the diameter in inches.

```
1 sound disc : analog, 33 1/3 rpm,
stereo. ; 12 in.

1 sound disc (49 min.) : digital,
stereo. ; 4 3/4 in.

1 computer disk : 3 1/2 in.
```

9) *Sound cassettes and cartridges.* Do not give dimensions.

10) *Three-dimensional objects.* Give the height, *or* the height and width, *or* the height, width, and depth (as appropriate) in centimetres.

```
1 sculpture : marble ; 110 cm. high

1 quilt : cotton, red & white ; 278 ×
200 cm.
```

If the object is in a container, name the container (for example, "in box") and add the dimensions of the container.

```
1 diorama ; in box 30 × 20 × 17 cm.
```

5E. Accompanying material

5E1. Definition. "Accompanying material" is material issued with, and intended to be used with, the bibliographic resource being catalogued. It is often, but not always, in a different physical form. Examples include: a slide set with an accompanying book; a book with an accompanying atlas; a filmstrip with an accompanying sound recording.

5E2. Give the number of physical units and the name of any significant accompanying material. Use the terms listed in rule 5B when possible.

```
323 p. : ill. ; 24 cm. + 6 maps

3 v. : ill. (some col.) ; 27 cm. + 1
set of teacher's notes

1 score ; 26 cm. + 1 sound cassette

1 filmstrip : col. ; 35 cm. + 1 sound
disc

1 computer optical disc : sd., col. ;
4 3/4 in. + 1 sound cassette
```

If the accompanying material is minor, *either* describe it in a note (see rule 7B10) *or* ignore it.

6. SERIES AREA

Contents:

6A. Preliminary rule
6B. Title proper of series
6C. Statements of responsibility relating to series
6D. Numbering within series
6E. Subseries
6F. More than one series

6A. Preliminary rule

6A1. Punctuation

Precede this area by a full stop, space, dash, space (. —).
Enclose each series statement in parentheses (( )).
Precede a statement of responsibility relating to a series by a space, diagonal slash, space (/).
Precede the numbering within a series by a space, semicolon, space (;).
Precede the title of a subseries by a full stop, space (.).

6A2. Sources of information. Take information recorded in this area from the bibliographic resource or its container. Do not give series information taken from any other source.

6B. Title proper of series

6B1. Transcribe the title proper of the series as found on the bibliographic resource or its container. See rule 1B for instructions on how to record titles proper.

> (About Britain ...[8]
>
> (Penguin crime fiction ...
>
> (A1 street atlas series ...
>
> (Family library of great music ...
>
> (Interactive digital computer teaching models ...

6B2. If more than one form of the series title is found on the bibliographic resource and its container, give the form found on the resource itself. If more than one form appears on the resource or if the variant forms appear only on the container, give the form that best identifies the series.

> (Carrier cookery cards ...
> (*appears on the item as:* Cookery cards *and as* Carrier cookery cards)

6C. Statements of responsibility relating to series

Only give statements of responsibility about persons or corporate bodies responsible for the series if they appear on the bibliographic resource or its container *and* if they are necessary to identify the series. See rule 1F for instructions on how to record statements of responsibility.

> (Works / Thomas Hardy ...
>
> (Sound cassettes / Institute for the New Age ...
>
> (Collected software / American University, English Language Institute ...

---

8. The three dots here and in the other examples in rule 6 indicate that other elements (for example, numbering) may be necessary to complete the series statement.

Do not record statements relating to editors of series.

> (Society and the Victorians ...
>
> *not*   (Society and the Victorians / general
> editor John Spiers ...

6D. Numbering within series

6D1. Give the numbering or other designation of the bibliographic resource within the series if that numbering appears on the item or its container. Give the numbering or other designation as it appears. Use standard abbreviations (for example, use "no." for "number" and "v." for "volume").

> (Collectors pieces ; 14)
>
> (VideoClassics ; 312)
>
> (Family library of great music ; album 5)
>
> (Computer simulation games ; module 5)
>
> (Sounds of the seventies ; no. 54)
>
> (Polyphony ; v. E)
>
> (Art and the modern world ; 1981A)

6E. Subseries

If the bibliographic resource is part of a series that is itself part of a larger series *and* both series are named on the resource or its container, give the details of the larger series before the details of the smaller series.

> (Science. The world environment)
>
> (Music for today. Series 2 ; no. 8)

6F. More than one series

If the bibliographic resource belongs to two or more separate series *and* both are named on the resource or its container, give the details of each series separately. Give the series statements in the order in which they appear.

> (Video marvels ; no. 33) (Educational
> progress series ; no. 3)

7. NOTE AREA

Contents:
    7A. Preliminary rule
    7B. Notes

7A. Preliminary rule

7A1. Give useful descriptive information that cannot be fitted into the rest of the description in a note. A general outline of types of notes is given in rule 7B. If a note seems to be useful, give it even if it is not in that general outline. When appropriate, combine two or more notes to make one note.

7A2. Punctuation

Precede each note by a full stop, space, dash, space (. —) *or* give each note as a separate paragraph (see rule 0D).

Separate any introductory word(s) of a note (for example, "Contents", "Summary") from the rest of the note by a colon, space (:).

7A3. Sources of information. Take notes from any suitable source.

7A4. Form of notes

Order. Give notes (if there is more than one note) in the order in which they are given in the general outline (see rule 7B).

References to other works. When referring to another work or bibliographic resource, give those of the following elements that are relevant:

```
Title / statement of responsibility.
Edition. Place : publisher, date.
```

Give them in that order and with that punctuation.

```
Revision of: Understand the law /
J.P. Smith. 3rd ed.

Originally published: London : Jampton
& Hardwycke, 1888

Facsimile reprint of: New ed.,
with additions. Oxford : Printed for
R. Clements, 1756
```

Formal notes. Use formal notes (those with the same introductory word(s)) if they can be easily understood and if they save space.

Informal notes. When writing your own notes, make them as brief and clear as possible.

7B. Notes

7B1. Special notes for serials and electronic resources

Frequency. If the resource being described is a serial, give the frequency of issue as the first note unless the frequency is obvious from the title (for example, "Annual report", "Monthly digest").

```
Annual

Weekly

Issued every month except August

Six issues yearly

Updated daily

Irregular
```

Note changes in frequency.

```
Weekly (1968-1981), monthly (1982-  )
```

Local electronic resources. System requirements. Always make a System requirements note when describing an electronic resource that is available locally. Give the make and model of the computer(s) on which it will run *and* any other system requirements that are important to its use (for example, amount of memory, name of the operating system, peripherals). Precede the note with "System requirements:".

```
System requirements: Macintosh

System requirements: UNIX workstation
with Mosaic software

System requirements: IBM PC; 64K;
colour card; 2 disk drives
```

Remote electronic resources. Mode of access. Always make a mode of access note for a remote electronic resource. Precede the note with "Mode of access:". If the mode of access is the Web, give the address.

> Mode of access: CSUNet
>
> Mode of access: Lexis system. Requires subscription
>
> Mode of access: World Wide Web www.ala.org

7B2. Nature of the item. Make a note giving the nature, scope, or artistic form of the bibliographic resource if it is not obvious from the rest of the description.

> Documentary
>
> Comedy in two acts
>
> Original recordings from 1921 to 1933
>
> Spreadsheet with word processing and graphics capabilities
>
> Interactive adventure game

7B3. Language. Make a note on the language(s) of the bibliographic resource if it is not obvious from the rest of the description.

> Commentary in English
>
> French dialogue, English subtitles

7B4. Adaptation. If the bibliographic resource is a manifestation of a work that is an adaptation of another work, make a note about the other work.

> Based on short stories by P.G. Wodehouse
>
> Spanish version of: Brushing away tooth decay
>
> Translation of: Dona Flor e seus dois maridos

7B5. Titles. Make notes on important titles borne by the bibliographic resource that are different from the title proper.

> Title on container: Butterflies and
> moths
>
> Disc 3 entitled: This amazing world

If the title of a serial or integrating resource varies slightly, say so.

> Title varies slightly

If each issue of a serial has an individual title, say so.

> Each issue has its own title

If you have supplied the title from other than the chief source of information, indicate the source.

> Title taken from: List of Chicago jazz
> recordings, 1940-1950 / B. McEnroe
>
> Title from script

Electronic resources. Always give the source of the title proper of an electronic resource.

> Title from title screen
>
> Title from CD-ROM label
>
> Title from title screen (viewed
> Jan. 20, 2003)
>
> Title based on contents viewed
> August 6, 2004

7B6. Credits and other statements of responsibility

Cast. List featured players, performers, narrators, or presenters.

> Presenter: Wallace Greenslade
>
> Cast: Diane Keaton, Woody Allen,
> Michael Murphy, Mariel Hemingway, Karen
> Ludwig, Meryl Streep

Credits. List persons (other than the cast) who have made an important contribution to the artistic or technical production of a motion picture, sound recording, videorecording, etc., and are not named in the statements of responsibility.

    Credits: Producer, Peter Rogers;
    director, Gerald Thomas

    Credits: Guitar and vocals, Eric
    Clapton; keyboards, Dick Sims; vocals,
    Marcy Levy; guitar, Georgy Terry; bass
    guitar, Carl Radle; drums, Jamie Oldaker

    Backing by the Amazing Lost Cowboys

    Piano: Gerald Moore

Other statements of responsibility. Give the names of any person(s) or body (bodies) not named in the statement of responsibility with an important connection with the bibliographic resource.

    Attributed to Aubrey Beardsley

    Based on music by Fats Waller

    Programmer, Leslie Larsen; reference
    manual, Oleg Kanjorski

    Systems designer, Henry James; sound,
    J&J Acoustics

7B7. Edition and history. If the bibliographic resource is a revision or reissue, make a note about the earlier item.

    Formerly available as: Those rockin'
    years

    Reprint of the August 30th 1938 issue

    Republished on the Internet, 2002

    Rev. ed. of: The portable Dorothy
    Parker

> Electronic version of the print
> publication, London : Fortune Press,
> 1956

Serials. Make a note linking the serial being described to another serial if it is continued by or continues another serial

> *or* is supplementary to another serial

> *or* has any other significant relationship to another serial.

> Continued by: The Irish history
> newsletter

> Continues: Bird watcher's gazette

> Supplement to: The daily collegian

> Absorbed: New society, 1988

Integrating resources. If the title of an integrating resource changes, give the earlier title(s).

> Former title: Washington newspapers
> database

7B8. Publication, etc. Give important details of the publication or distribution of the bibliographic resource that cannot be given in the publication, etc., area.

> Distributed in Canada by: West Coast
> Enterprises

> Journal first issued in the mid 1960s,
> ceased publication in 1981 or 1982

7B9. Physical details. Give important physical details that cannot be given in the physical description area.

> Magnetic sound track

> In two containers

> Collage of wood, fabric, & paper

> Unmounted

> Pattern: Fannie's fan

```
Distributed as a Zip file

Database also on CD-ROM

Still image compressed using JPEG
```

7B10. Accompanying material and supplements. Give important information about accompanying and supplementary material that cannot be given elsewhere in the description.

```
Consists of clear plastic model
and accompanying tape/slide set and
instructional booklet (16 p.)

Set includes booklet: The Dada
influence. 32 p.

Slides with every 7th issue

Sunday issue includes magazine
supplement
```

7B11. Audience. If the intended audience bibliographic resource is not apparent from the rest of the description, state it here.

```
Intended audience: Grades 3-5

For adolescents

Intended audience: Post-graduate
engineering students
```

7B12. Other formats available. Give details of other formats in which the content of the bibliographic resource has been issued.

```
Issued also on cassette tape

Issued also as cassette (VHS)

Online version of the print publication:
Icarus

Also issued electronically via World
Wide Web in PDF format
```

7B13. Summary. Give a brief summary of the content of a bibliographic resource if it is required by the policy of your library.

> Summary: Melissa and her friends
> discover a hidden treasure and defeat a
> gang that wants to steal it

> Summary: Episodes from the novel about
> a corrupt library administrator, read by
> the author

> Summary: A brief historical account of
> the discovery of antibiotics

> Summary: A reading exercise presenting
> some aspects of Native American culture

> Summary: An interactive multimedia tool
> for studying the human anatomy

7B14. Contents. If the bibliographic resource consists of a number of
named parts, list those parts in the order in which they occur if the
policy of the library requires such listings. Separate the names of the
parts by a space, dash, space (—).

> Contents: Polonaise in F sharp minor,
> op. 44 -- Polonaise in A flat, op. 53 --
> Polonaise in A, op. 40, no. 1 --
> Nocturne, op. 27, no. 1 -- Etude, op.
> 10, no. 3 -- Mazurka in B flat, op. 7,
> no. 1

> Contents: Queen Lucia -- The male
> impersonator -- Lucia in London

> Contents: Trent's last case -- Trent's
> own case / with H. Warner Allan -- Trent
> intervenes

> Contents: CD-ROM data (1:29) -- The
> young person's guide to the orchestra
> (16:27) -- Extra audio examples (55:43)

If the bibliographic resource contains an important part that is not evident from the rest of the description, note that here.

> ```
> Includes some poems
> ```
> (*title is:* Collected prose works)
>
> ```
> Includes three études and two mazurkas
> ```
> (*title is:* Chopin's polonaises)
>
> ```
> Includes bibliographical references
> ```

7B15. Copy being described, library's holdings, and restrictions on use. Make notes on:

a) important descriptive details of the copy being described

> ```
> Library's set lacks slides 7, 8, and 9
>
> Library's copy signed by the author
> ```

b) your library's holdings of an incomplete multipart resource

> ```
> Library has vol. 1 and vols. 3-8
> ```

c) any restrictions on use.

> ```
> Available to faculty and graduate
> students only
>
> Resource closed until March 6th, 2011
> ```

7B16. "With" notes. If the bibliographic resource being catalogued lacks a collective title *and* the title given in the title and statement of responsibility area applies to only part of that resource (see rule 1G) because you are making a separate entry for each of the parts of the item, make a note beginning "With:" and listing the titles of the other parts in the order in which they occur.

> ```
> With: Symphony no. 5 / Beethoven (side B)
>
> With: Aimless love / J.M. Morgan --
> Headwinds / Joe M. Philipson
> ```

7B17. Serials, integrating resources, and multipart resources: basis for the description. If the first issue of a serial, first iteration of an integrating resource, or first part of a multipart bibliographic resource is not the basis for the description, give details of the issue, iteration, or part that is. For remote access resources, always give the date on which the resource was viewed.

```
Description based on: Vol. 5, no. 1
(March/April 1997)

Description based on printout of screen
display of: Vol. 17, no. 1 (Mar. 1994)

Description based on home page dated
August 9, 1998

Description based on source viewed
September 2, 2003
```

8. STANDARD NUMBER

Contents:
    8A.   Preliminary rule
    8B.   Standard number

8A. Preliminary rule

8A1. Punctuation

Precede this area by a full stop, space, dash, space (. —) *or* start a new paragraph (see rule 0D).

8A2. Sources of information. Take standard numbers from any suitable source.

8B. Standard number

8B1. Give the International Standard Book Number (ISBN), or International Standard Serial Number (ISSN), or any other internationally agreed standard number of the bibliographic resource being described. Precede that number with the standard abbreviation (ISBN, ISSN, etc.) and use standard hyphenation.

```
ISBN 0-8389-3346-7

ISSN 0002-9869
```

8B2. If the resource has more than one such number, give the one that applies specifically to the entity being described.

> ISBN 0-379-00550-6
>> (*this is the ISBN for the set being described; volume 1 also carries an ISBN for that volume; do not record it*)

9. SUPPLEMENTARY ITEMS

9A. Supplementary bibliographic resources described independently

If a supplementary bibliographic resource has its own title *and* can be used independently, make a separate description. Link it to the bibliographic resource to which it is supplementary by making a note (see rule 7B7).

> Hye sharzhoom : the newspaper of the
> California State University, Fresno
> Armenian Students Organization and
> Armenian Studies Program. -- Vol. 2,
> no. 1 (Nov. 1979)-. -- Fresno : Armenian
> Studies Program, CSUF, 1978-
> v. : ill. ; 44 cm.
> Quarterly
> Title also appears in Armenian script
> Vol. 1 consisted of unnumbered "special
> issues"
> Supplement to: The daily collegian

9B. Supplementary bibliographic resources described dependently

If a supplementary bibliographic resource has no independent title *or* cannot be used independently:

> *either* record it as accompanying material (see rule 5E)

>> 5 v. : ill. ; 32 cm. + 1 v.

> *or* make a note (see rule 7B10).

>> *Note:* Accompanied by supplement (37 p.)
>> issued in 1969

10. RESOURCES MADE UP OF MORE THAN ONE TYPE OF MATERIAL

10A. Apply this rule to bibliographic resources that are made up of two or more parts, two or more of which belong to separate material types (for example, a book and a sound recording).

10B. If the resource has a main component, make a description based on that main component and give details of the secondary component(s):

> *either* as accompanying material (see rule 5E)

```
47 slides : col. + 1 sound tape
reel
```

> *or* in a note (see rule 7B10).

```
3 v. : ill. ; 30 cm.
Note: Sound disc (12 min. : digital,
stereo. ; 4 3/4 in.) in pocket at
end of v. 3
```

10C. If the resource has no one main component, follow the rules below as well as the other rules in this part.

10C1. General material designation. If you are using general material designations (see rule 1C), *and* the bibliographic resource has a collective title, give "[kit]".

```
Multisensory experience for the
preschooler [kit]
```

If the resource has no collective title, give the appropriate designation after each title.

```
Telling the time [filmstrip].  The
story of time [sound recording]
```

10C2. Physical description. *Either* give separate physical descriptions for each part or group of parts belonging to each distinct class of material, starting a new paragraph with each physical description

```
Tomato growing [kit] : a multimedia
presentation / concept, Dion Garber ;
```

```
programmer, Trev Baxter. -- Dallas :
Thraxton Multimedia, 1997
   46 slides : col.
   1 sound disc (15 min.) : digital,
stereo. ; 4 3/4 in.
   1 electronic disk : col. ; 3 1/2 in.
   (AgriMedia ; A32)
```

or give a general term as the statement of extent for bibliographic resources with a large number of different materials. Add the number of pieces if that number can be ascertained easily.

```
   various pieces

   36 pieces
```

10C3. Notes. Make notes on each of the particular parts as the first note(s).

```
   Tape cassette also available as
   disc. -- Slides photographed in Death
   Valley, Calif.
```

11. FACSIMILES, PHOTOCOPIES, AND OTHER REPRODUCTIONS

In describing a facsimile, photocopy, or other reproduction in eye-readable or microform, describe the facsimile, etc., and not the original. Give data relating to the original in a single note.

```
   Demos : a story of English socialism /
   George Gissing ; edited with an introduction
   by Pierre Coustillas. -- Brighton, Sussex
   : Harvester Press, 1972.
      477 p. ; 23 cm. -- (Society and the
   Victorians)
      Facsimile reprint of: New ed. London :
   Smith Elder, 1897
```

Alice's adventures under ground / by
Lewis Carroll. -- New York : Dover, 1965.
   91 p. : ill. ; 22 cm.
Complete facsimile of the British
Museum manuscript of: Alice's adventures
under ground

PART 2

Headings, Uniform Titles, and References

Introduction

When you have made a standard description according to rules 0-11, add access points (name headings and/or titles) in accordance with the rules in this part to that description to create a catalogue entry. The rules that follow deal with the choice of access points (21–29), with their form (30–61), and with the making of references (62–65). General rules precede specific rules. If you cannot find an appropriate specific rule, use the preceding general rule.

The rules in this part apply to all forms of library materials (printed, audiovisual, electronic, etc.) and to monographic, serial, and integrating resources.

Rules 40–43, 46B, and 51 deal with additions to access points. Always make these additions (if possible) if they are necessary to differentiate between otherwise identical access points in the same catalogue. For example:

```
Robertson, John, 1903-1971

Robertson, John, 1918-
```

If you wish, make such additions even if they are not needed now, so that future conflicts can be avoided.

As in rules 0–11, the examples in the following rules are supposed only to illustrate the rule, not to add to it. In cases of doubt, always prefer the rule as guidance rather than the examples.

The presentation of examples is intended to help you to understand the rules. It is not intended to imply a certain form of presentation in your catalogue. The transcriptions from the source of information are set out in ISBD style (see part 1). In a few instances (see, for example, rule 25C2), more information than is required for a standard description is included to demonstrate the rule fully.

Choice of Access Points

Contents

21. INTRODUCTION

21A. Main and added entries

Use rules 23–29 to decide the access points (name headings and/or titles) that are to be added to the bibliographic description (see rules 0–11) so that the description can be added to, and retrieved from, a catalogue.

Use rules 23–28 to decide which access point is the heading for the main entry (other access points being headings for added entries). If, however, your library does not distinguish between main entries and added entries, treat all access points as equal and use rules 23–29 to tell you which and how many access points to make.

Generally, each rule and its example(s) only cover certain added-entry access points. Additional added-entry access points (for example, series and title headings) may be required by the general rule on added entries (see rule 29).

21B. Sources for determining access points

Prefer the chief source of information (see rule 0A) to other sources, but also take into account any relevant information found elsewhere on the bibliographic resource and, when necessary, in accompanying material and reference sources.

21C. Form of examples

The examples in rules 24–29 indicate only the access points to be made without showing their complete form. Use rules 30–61 to establish the complete form.

When an example is followed by "Main entry under title" or "Added entry under title", it usually means the title proper (see rule 1B). In a few cases it may mean the uniform title (see rules 57–61).

22. CHANGES IN TITLES PROPER

22A. Definition

Except for multipart resources (see rule 22B) and integrating resources (see rule 22D), make a new catalogue entry for a work if its title changes (see rule 22C). A title proper has changed if:

1) any word other than an article (for example, "the," "a," "le"), a preposition (for example, "to," "de," "of "), or a conjunction (for example, "and," "but," "aber") is added, deleted, or changed

or

2) there is a change in the order of the first five words (six if the title begins with an article).

However, do not make a new catalogue entry if the change is:

1) in the representation of a word or words (for example, ignore a change from "Trout and salmon news" to "Trout & salmon news")

2) after the first five words (six if the first is an article) and does not change the meaning of the title (for example, ignore a change from "The journal of the antiquities of Bootle and surroundings" to "The journal of the antiquities of Bootle and its environs")

3) the addition or deletion of the name of the issuing body at the end of the title (for example, ignore a change from "The

journal of the cuisine of provincial Indiana of the League of
Hoosier Gourmets" to "The journal of the cuisine of provincial
Indiana")

or

4) the addition, deletion, or change of punctuation (for example,
   ignore a change from "Boot, shoe, sandal news" to "Boot/
   shoe/sandal news".

22B. Monographs

If the title proper of a monograph in more than one physical part (for
example, a multivolume book) changes from one part to another, use
the title proper of the first part as the title proper of the whole monograph. Make a note (see rule 7B5) about the other title(s).

```
   The romance of the tomato : a seven
part instructional film / devised and
presented by Gervase Scudamore. --
London : Hamberger & Pollock, 1987
   7 film cassettes (20 min. each) : sd.,
col. ; standard 8 mm.
   Cassettes 6 and 7 entitled: The tomato
and you
```

22C. Serials

If the title proper of a serial changes, make a separate main entry for
each title. Link these entries with notes (see rule 7B7).

22D. Integrating resources

If the title proper of an integrating resource changes, replace the
former title proper with the new title proper. Give the earlier title in a
note (see rule 7B7).

23. GENERAL RULE

23A. Works of personal authorship

23A1. Definition. A personal author is the person who is chiefly
responsible for the content of a work. Examples are:

> writers of texts
> composers of music
> artists (sculptors, painters, etc.)
> photographers
> compilers of bibliographies
> cartographers (makers of maps)
> creators of electronic resources

In some cases (see rule 27B1g), treat performers as the authors of sound recordings.

23A2. Enter a work by one person under the heading for that person (see rule 24A).

Enter a work by two or more persons under:

> the principal personal author (see rule 25B1)

or

> the person named first (see rules 25B2, 25C1, and 27)

or

> its title (see rules 25C2 and 26B).

Make added entries as instructed in rule 29.

23B. Entry under corporate body

23B1. Definition. A corporate body is an organization or group of persons that has a name. If you are in doubt as to whether words indicating a particular body constitute a name, treat them as a name if they have initial capital letters *and/or* if they begin with the definite article (for example, "The," "Le"). For example, "The British Museum" is a name and "a group of concerned citizens" is not; "The Modern Jazz Quartet" is a name and "seven rock superstars" is not. In other cases of doubt, do not regard the phrase as a name.

Examples of corporate bodies are:

> business firms
> governments (local and national)
> government agencies (local and national)
> churches
> associations (for example, clubs, societies)
> institutions (for example, museums, libraries, schools)

> international agencies
> conferences
> exhibitions, expeditions, and festivals
> performing groups

Some corporate bodies are subordinate to (part of) other bodies. For example, the Henry Madden Library is a part of the California State University, Fresno; the Home Office is part of the government of the United Kingdom.

23B2. Enter a work issued by a corporate body or originating from a corporate body under the heading for that body (see rule 24B) if it is one or more of the following:

a) an administrative work dealing with:

> the corporate body itself (for example, an annual report)

> *or* its policies, procedures, operations, etc. (for example, a policy statement, a staff manual)

> *or* its finances (for example, a budget, a financial report)

> *or* its personnel (for example, a staff list)

> *or* its resources or possessions (for example, a catalogue, an inventory, a membership directory)

b) a law or collection of laws, an administrative regulation, a treaty *(for detailed guidance on these materials, see the full* AACR2)

c) a report of a committee, commission, etc. (provided that the report states the opinion of the committee, etc., and does not merely describe a situation objectively)

d) a liturgical text for which a particular church, denomination, etc., is responsible *(for detailed guidance on these materials, see the full* AACR2)

e) a collection of papers given at a conference (provided that the conference is named in the item being catalogued); the report of an expedition (provided that the expedition is named in the item being catalogued)

f) a sound recording, videorecording, or film created *and* performed by a group

g) a map or other cartographic material created by a corporate body.

If such a work originates from two or more bodies, see also rules 25–27.

If a work does not fall into one of the types listed above, or if you are in doubt about whether it does, enter it under a person's name or under title as appropriate. In addition, make added entries under the names of prominently named corporate bodies as instructed in rule 29B2e.

23C. Entry under title

Enter a work under its title when:

1) the author is unknown *and* no corporate body is responsible (see rule 23B2)
2) the work has more than three authors *and* none of them is the principal author (see rule 25C2) *and* no corporate body is responsible (see rule 23B2)
3) it is a collection *and* has a collective title (see rule 26B)
4) it is not by a person or persons *and* is issued by a corporate body *but* is not one of the types of publication listed in rule 23B2
5) it is a sacred scripture (such as the Bible, the Koran, or the Talmud) *or* an ancient anonymous work (such as *Beowulf* or the *Arabian nights*).

24. WORKS FOR WHICH ONE PERSON OR CORPORATE BODY IS RESPONSIBLE

24A. Works by one person

Enter a work by one person under the heading for that person even if he or she is not named in the bibliographic resource being catalogued.

> The good soldier / by Ford Madox Ford
> *Main entry under the heading for Ford*

> I.F. Stone's newsletter
> *Main entry under the heading for Stone*

```
Wavelength / Van Morrison
```
   (*a sound recording composed, produced, and
   performed by Morrison*)
Main entry under the heading for Morrison

```
Don Quixote
```
   (*a print by Picasso*)
Main entry under the heading for Picasso

```
Collins Italian gem dictionary :
Italian-English, English-Italian /
Isopel May
```
Main entry under the heading for May

```
Newts in the wild : London ponds /
made by Norma McEachern
```
   (*a filmstrip*)
Main entry under the heading for McEachern

```
Ecstasy and me : my life as a woman /
Hedy Lamarr
```
   (*the "ghosted" autobiography of a movie star,
   "ghost-writer" not named*)
Main entry under the heading for Lamarr

Enter a collection of, or selections from, works by one person under the heading for that person even if she or he is not named in the bibliographic resource being catalogued.

```
The Brandenburg concertos / J.S. Bach
```
Main entry under the heading for Bach

```
The poems of John Keats / edited by
Jack Stillinger
```
Main entry under the heading for Keats

```
The sweet singer of Penge
```
   (*a collection of poems published anonymously but
   known to be by Eric Lancaster*)
Main entry under the heading for Lancaster

```
Selected essays / George Orwell
```
Main entry under the heading for Orwell

24B. Works for which one corporate body is responsible

If a work originating from a single corporate body falls into one or more of the categories listed in rule 23B2, enter it under the heading for the body.

Entry under corporate heading

    Administrative works

> Annual report of the Institute for the Furtherance of Psychic Studies
> *Main entry under the heading for the Institute*

> Additions to the Library / H.D. Timpson Library, Branksome
> *Main entry under the heading for the Library*

> Rules and regulations of the Chicago Board of Trade
> *Main entry under the heading for the Board*

    Laws, etc.

> The health and safety at work act 1974
>   (*a British law*)
> *Main entry under the heading for the United Kingdom*

> Rules, regulations, and by-laws relating to the storage and sale of fish / City of Minneapolis
> *Main entry under the heading for Minneapolis*

    Committee, etc., reports

> Report and recommendation to the Governor and the General Assembly / Illinois Commission on the Status of Women
>   (*a serial*)
> *Main entry under the heading for the Commission*

```
      Hartford Civic Center Coliseum roof
collapse : final report / Common Council
Committee to Investigate the Coliseum
Roof Failure
```
Main entry under the heading for the Committee

Liturgical works

```
      Rite of marriage. -- Washington :
United States Catholic Conference
```
Main entry under the heading for the Catholic Church

Conference, etc., proceedings

```
      Abstracts of the annual meeting /
Free Thought Society
```
Main entry under the heading for the Society's meeting

```
      Proceedings / Conference on the
Mass Media and the Black Community,
Cincinnati, 1969 ; sponsored by the
Pen and Paper Club of Cincinnati
```
Main entry under the heading for the Conference

Works created and performed by a group

```
      Bridges to Babylon / the Rolling Stones
```
      (a sound recording composed, produced, and
      performed by the rock group)
Main entry under the heading for the group

```
      Free South Africa! : an improvisational
video performance / the Children of the
Universe
```
Main entry under the heading for the group

Maps created and published by a corporate body

```
      Fresno & Fresno County. -- Modesto, Ca.
: Compass Maps, 1986
```
Main entry under the heading for Compass Maps

Entry not under corporate heading

> Italians in America / made and released by the Anti-Defamation League of B'nai B'rith
>
> (*a filmstrip*)
> *Main entry under title*
> *Added entry under the heading for the League*

> Symphony no. 8 in B minor (Unfinished) / Schubert
>
> (*a sound recording by the Philadelphia Orchestra*)
> *Main entry under the heading for Schubert*
> *Added entry under the heading for the Orchestra*

> Bulletin / Pinner Ornithological Society
> *Main entry under title*
> *Added entry under the heading for the Society*

> California library directory : listings for public, academic, special, state agency, and county law libraries / Library Development Services Bureau, California State Library
> *Main entry under title*
> *Added entry under the heading for the Bureau*

> Costs and revenue of national newspapers / National Board for Prices and Incomes
> *Main entry under title*
> *Added entry under the heading for the Board*

> Near Eastern art in Chicago collections / the Art Institute of Chicago, November 17, 1973-January 20, 1974
>
> (*a catalogue of an exhibition*)
> *Main entry under title*
> *Added entry under the heading for the Institute*

```
The political lighthouse / owned,
operated, and maintained by Starlight
```
(*an electronic resource*)
Main entry under title
Added entry under the heading for Starlight

25. WORKS FOR WHICH TWO OR MORE PERSONS OR CORPORATE BODIES ARE RESPONSIBLE

25A. Scope

Apply this rule to:

1) works produced by two or more persons (joint authors, collaborators, etc.)
2) works for which two or more persons have prepared separate contributions (including the records of debates and discussions)
3) works consisting of letters, etc., exchanged by two or more persons
4) works issued by, or originating from, two or more corporate bodies *and* that fall into one or more of the categories listed in rule 23B2.

For works consisting of collections of, or selections from, already existing works (such as anthologies), see rule 26.

For special types of collaboration, see rule 27.

25B. Principal responsibility indicated

25B1. If the layout or wording of the chief source of information of a bibliographic resource that is a manifestation of a work by two or more persons or bodies indicates clearly that one person or body is chiefly responsible, enter under the heading for that person or body. Make added entries under the headings for the other persons or bodies if there are not more than two of them.

```
The Taylor system in Franklin
management : application and results /
by George D. Babcock in collaboration
with Reginald Trautschold
```
Main entry under the heading for Babcock
Added entry under the heading for Trautschold

> Unknown horizons : visions of the
> distant future : a video experience /
> Maude LaFarge with the help of Simon,
> Paul, and Janette
> *Main entry under the heading for LaFarge*

> Technical services in libraries :
> acquisitions, cataloging, classification,
> binding, photographic reproduction, and
> circulation operations / by
> Maurice F. Tauber and associates
>> (*the seven associates are named on the leaf following*
>> *the title leaf*)
> *Main entry under the heading for Tauber*

25B2. If two or three persons or bodies are shown as being principally responsible, enter under the heading for the one named first. Make added entries under the headings for the others.

> Elementary differential equations
> with linear algebra / Ross L. Finney,
> Donald R. Ostberg with the assistance
> of Robert G. Kuller
> *Main entry under the heading for Finney*
> *Added entry under the heading for Ostberg*

25C. Principal responsibility not indicated

25C1. If, in the case of a work by two or three persons or bodies, no one person or body is clearly principally responsible (see rule 25B), enter under the heading for the one named first. Make added entries under the headings for the others.

> Women artists, the twentieth century /
> authors Karen Petersen, J.J. Wilson
>> (*a slide set*)
> *Main entry under the heading for Petersen*
> *Added entry under the heading for Wilson*

```
The basement tapes / Bob Dylan & the Band
```
   (*sound recording of songs written and performed by
   Dylan and the rock group the Band*)
Main entry under the heading for Dylan
Added entry under the heading for the Band

```
PolicyWonk.com : tools and resources
for policy mavens / by Shane Heiser and
Ken Zimmerman
```
Main entry under the heading for Heiser
Added entry under the heading for Zimmerman

```
General college mathematics / W.L.
Ayres, Cleota G. Fry, H.F.S. Jonah
```
Main entry under the heading for Ayres
Added entries under the headings for Fry and Jonah

25C2. If, in the case of a work by four or more persons or bodies, none of the persons or bodies is clearly principally responsible (see rule 25B), enter under the title. Make an added entry under the heading for the first person or body named in the chief source of information.

```
Outlaw country / Willie Nelson, Waylon
Jennings, David Allan Coe, Hank Williams, Jr.
```
   (*sound recording; all four performers named on
   the labels*)
Main entry under title
Added entry under the heading for Nelson

```
The art of Gauguin / Richard Brettell,
Françoise Cachin, Claire Fréches-Thory,
Charles F. Stuckey
```
   (*exhibition catalogue; all four authors named on
   title page*)
Main entry under title
Added entry under the heading for Brettell

```
The modern age / edited by Boris Ford
```
   (*essays by various people produced under the
   editorship of Ford*)
Main entry under title
Added entry under the heading for Ford

26. COLLECTIONS OF WORKS BY DIFFERENT PERSONS OR BODIES

26A. Scope

Apply this rule to:

1) collections of independent works, or extracts from individual works, by different persons or bodies (for example, anthologies)
2) works consisting partly of independent works and partly of contributions by different persons or bodies.

Do not apply this rule to works covered by rule 23B2 (for example, conference proceedings).

26B. With collective title

If a bibliographic resource belongs to one of the types listed in rule 26A *and* has its own collective title, enter it under that title.

If the resource has one, two, or three editors or compilers named in the chief source of information, make added entries under the headings for each of them. If there are four or more editors or compilers named in the chief source of information, make an added entry under the heading for the one named first.

> The new Oxford book of English light verse / chosen by Kingsley Amis
> *Main entry under title*
> *Added entry under the heading for Amis*

> The family of man ... / created by Edward Steichen
> (*collection of 503 photographs by various people*)
> *Main entry under title*
> *Added entry under the heading for Steichen*

> Why a duck? : visual and verbal gems from the Marx Brothers movies / edited by Richard J. Anobile
> *Main entry under title*
> *Added entry under the heading for Anobile*

26C. Without collective title

If a bibliographic resource belongs to one of the types listed in rule 26A *and* has no collective title, enter it under the heading for the first work named in the chief source of information. If the resource lacks a chief source of information, enter it under the heading for the first work in the item.

Make added entries under the headings for editors, compilers, and/or contributors as instructed in rule 26B.

Make an analytical added entry (see 29B8) for each of the works in such a resource.

```
A John Field suite / Harty.  A dance
in the sunshine / Bax.  A Shropshire
lad, etc. / Butterworth.  There is a
willow grows aslant a brook / Bridge
```
Main entry under the heading for Harty
Added entries (name/title; see rule 29B4) under the headings
for Bax, Butterworth, and Bridge

27. WORKS OF MIXED RESPONSIBILITY

27A. Scope

A work of mixed responsibility is one that involves the collaboration of two or more persons or bodies (see rule 23B2 for cases in which a corporate body is responsible) *and* to which the persons and/or bodies make different kinds of contribution. Examples of the different kinds of contribution are: writing, adapting, illustrating, editing, arranging, translating, and performing.

Typical instances of mixed responsibility are:

> a work with text by one person and illustrations by another
>
> a work created by one person and adapted by another
>
> a work by one person with a commentary by another
>
> a work by one person translated by another
>
> a law for which a corporate body is responsible with a
>   commentary by a person
>
> an electronic resource created by one person with software
>   written by another

a musical work by one person arranged by another

a musical work by one person performed by another person or by a performing group.

This rule divides all cases of mixed responsibility into two types. These are:

1) modifications of existing works (see rule 27B)
2) new works produced by the collaboration of different persons and/or bodies making different intellectual or artistic contributions (see rule 27C).

27B. Modifications of existing works

27B1. Enter a work that is a modification of an existing work under the heading for the new work and make a name/title added entry (see rule 29B4) for the original work *if* the nature and content of the original has been changed substantially *or if* the medium of expression has changed.
Examples of such change are:

a) paraphrases, rewritings, adaptations for children, and versions in a different literary form of written works

> Jump! : the adventures of Brer Rabbit / by Joel Chandler Harris ; adapted by Van Dyke Parks and Malcolm Jones
> (*adaptation of Harris's* Adventures of Brer Rabbit)
> *Main entry under the heading for Parks*
> *Added entry under the heading for Jones*
> *Added entry (name/title) under the heading for Harris*

> Robert Fitzgerald reads from his Iliad
> (*sound recording, read by the poet, of his modern version of Homer's* Iliad)
> *Main entry under the heading for Fitzgerald*
> *Added entry (name/title) under the heading for Homer*

b) revisions of texts when the reviser(s) is named in the chief source *and* the original author(s) *either* is no longer named in the title and statement of responsibility area *or* is named only in the title proper

```
The law of Ireland / G. Fenn
```
("a complete revision of Innes and Montgomery's Irish
law"—*title page*)
Main entry under the heading for Fenn
Added entry (name/title) under the heading for Innes

```
Roget's Thesaurus of English words and
phrases. -- New ed. / completely revised
and modernized by Robert A. Dutch
```
Main entry under the heading for Dutch
Added entry (name/title) under the heading for Roget

c) commentaries when the bibliographic resource is presented as a
commentary

```
The Theaetetus of Plato: a commentary /
by Spenser Sayers
```
    (*contains the Greek text of the* Theaetetus)
Main entry under the heading for Sayers
Added entry (name/title) under the heading for Plato

d) adaptations of graphic art works from one medium of the
graphic arts to another

```
Courbet's The painter's studio / an
engraving by M.M.C.
```
Main entry under the heading for M.M.C.
Added entry (name/title) under the heading for Courbet

e) reproductions of art works with text when the writer of the text
is represented as the author of the work in the chief source of
information

```
William Morris wallpapers and chintzes
/ Fiona Clark
```
    (*reproductions of Morris's designs with an annotated*
    catalogue by Clark)
Main entry under the heading for Clark
Added entry under the heading for Morris

f) alterations (free transcriptions, etc.), paraphrases, and variations of musical works

Rhapsody on a theme by Paganini : for
piano and orchestra / Rachmaninov
Main entry under the heading for Rachmaninov
Added entry under the heading for Paganini

g) sound recordings of works by different persons performed by a
principal performer or performers[1]

Contrary to ordinary / Jerry Jeff Walker
(*ten songs, each by a different composer, performed by*
Walker)
Main entry under the heading for Walker

James Galway plays Song of the seashore
and other melodies of Japan
(*compositions by various Japanese composers,*
performed by Galway)
Main entry under the heading for Galway

The fine art of surfacing / the
Boomtown Rats
(*songs, by various members of the band, performed by*
a rock group)
Main entry under the heading for the band

h) novels, etc., based on motion pictures, television shows, etc.

Star wars: the novel of the smash hit
movie / by E.B. Knowles
Main entry under the heading for Knowles
Added entry under the heading for the motion picture

The laugh was on Lazarus: a novel
based on the ABC television series The
avengers / John Garforth
Main entry under the heading for Garforth
Added entry under the heading for the television series

---

1. Consider such a sound recording to have a principal performer or principal performers when the wording, layout, typography, etc., of the chief source of information clearly present the activity of the performer(s) as the major purpose of the
recording.

i) motion pictures, television shows, electronic resources, etc., based on novels and other texts.

> The charmer / by Allan Prior
> > (*six-part television play based on Patrick Hamilton's novel* Mr. Stimpson and Mr. Gorse)
>
> *Main entry under title*
> *Added entries (name/title) under the headings for Prior and*
> > *Hamilton*

> Romeo & Juliet / producer Chris Jennings. -- Version 1.00c
> > (*an electronic interactive multimedia resource based on the Shakespeare play*)
>
> *Main entry under title*
> *Added entry under the heading for Jennings*
> *Added entry (name/title) under the heading for Shakespeare*

27B2. Enter any other modification of an existing work under the heading for the original work.

Examples of modifications entered under the headings for the original works are:

a) musical works by one person performed by another

> Willie Nelson sings Kris Kristofferson
> > (*songs by Kristofferson, performed by Nelson*)
>
> *Main entry under the heading for Kristofferson*
> *Added entry under the heading for Nelson*

b) translations

> Twenty love poems and a song of despair / Pablo Neruda ; translated by W.S. Merwin
> *Main entry under the heading for Neruda*
> *Added entry under the heading for Merwin (see rule 29B6)*

> True history ; and Lucius, or, The ass / Lucian ; translated from the Greek by Paul Turner
> *Main entry under the heading for Lucian*

Added entry (name/title; see rule 29B8) under the heading
  for Lucian for Lucius, or, The ass
Added entry under the heading for Turner (see rule 29B6)

c) arrangements of musical works

```
Original motion picture soundtrack, The
sting / featuring the music of Scott
Joplin ; adapted and arranged by Marvin
Hamlisch
```
Main entry under the heading for Joplin
Added entry under the heading for Hamlisch

d) texts with commentary when the item is presented as an edition of the text

```
Plato's Republic : with a commentary /
by Roderick Wolfe
```
Main entry under the heading for Plato
Added entry under the heading for Wolfe

e) abridgements of, and excerpts from, existing works

```
Great scenes from Pickwick
```
  (*excerpts from Dickens'* Pickwick papers)
Main entry under the heading for Dickens

```
My life with Sherlock Holmes :
conversations in Baker Street / edited
by J.R. Hamilton
```
  (*selections from Arthur Conan Doyle's Sherlock*
  Holmes stories)
Main entry under the heading for Doyle
Added entry under the heading for Hamilton

f) illustrated works.

```
The world of Pooh : the complete Winnie-
the-Pooh and The house at Pooh Corner /
by A.A. Milne ; with decorations and new
illustrations in full colour by E.H. Shepard
```
Main entry under the heading for Milne
Added entry under the heading for Shepard (see rule 29B6)

27C. New works produced by persons or bodies making different intellectual or artistic contributions

Enter a work produced by two or more persons or bodies making different intellectual or artistic contributions under the heading for the person or body given prominence by the wording or layout of the chief source of information of the bibliographic resource being catalogued. If there are two or three collaborating persons or bodies, make an added entry under the heading(s) for the other(s).

If no one person or body is given prominence *and* there are two or three persons or bodies named, enter under the heading for the person or body named first in the chief source. Make an added entry under the heading(s) for the other(s).

If no one person or body is given prominence *and* there are more than three persons or bodies named, enter under title. Make an added entry under the heading for the person or body named first.

> Goodbye baby & amen : a saraband for
> the sixties / David Bailey & Peter Evans
>   *(photographs by Bailey, text by Evans)*
> *Main entry under the heading for Bailey*
> *Added entry under the heading for Evans*

> Duffy and the devil : a Cornish tale /
> retold by Harve Zemach ; with pictures
> by Margot Zemach
> *Main entry under the heading for H. Zemach*
> *Added entry under the heading for M. Zemach*

28. RELATED WORKS

28A. Scope

Apply this rule to a separately catalogued work that has a relationship to another separately catalogued work.

Typical examples of related works are:

> continuations and sequels
> supplements

indexes
concordances
screenplays, scenarios, etc.
collections of extracts from serials
subseries
special numbers of serials

For adaptations, revisions, translations, etc., see rule 27.

28B. Enter a related work under its own heading according to the rules on entry (rules 23–27). Make the appropriate added entries according to those rules and rule 29.

Make an added entry under the name heading *or* name/title (see rule 29B4) *or* title, as appropriate, of the work(s) to which it is related.

```
Colonel Sun / Robert Markham
```
   (*a sequel to Ian Fleming's series of James Bond novels*)
   Main entry under the heading for Markham
   Added entry under the heading for Fleming

```
Index of characters and events in the
Pickwick papers / Nigel Appleby
```
   (*an index to the novel by Dickens*)
   Main entry under the heading for Appleby
   Added entry (name/title) under the heading for Dickens

```
Blue / writers, Meade Roberts,
Ronald M. Cohen
```
   (*the screenplay of the motion picture* Blue)
   Main entry under the heading for Roberts
   *Added entries under the headings for Cohen and the motion
      picture*

```
English art, 1970: a special number of
Eclectic art review
```
   Main entry under title
   Added entry under Eclectic art review

Alice's wonders / adapted from "Alice
in Wonderland" by Wilford Hagers
> (*a computer program based on the Lewis Carroll work*)
> *Main entry under the heading for Hagers*
> *Added entry (name/title) under the heading for Carroll*

Writing for love or money : thirty-five
essays reprinted from the Saturday review
of literature
Main entry under title
Added entry under Saturday review of literature

Carleton journalism review
> (*distributed with* Content: Canada's national news
> media magazine)
> *Main entry under title*
> *Added entry under* Content

29. ADDED ENTRIES

29A. General rule

29A1. Scope. Rule 29 gives general guidance on the making of added entries. Use it to supplement the specific instructions in rules 23–28.

29A2. Make an added entry under the heading for a person or corporate body or under a title if some users of the catalogue might look under that heading or title rather than under the main entry heading. If in doubt as to whether to make an added entry, make it.

29A3. Construct a heading for an added entry according to the instructions in rules 30–61.

For instructions on name/title added entry headings, see rule 29B4.

29A4. If the reason for an added entry is not apparent from the description (for example, if a person or body used as the basis for an added entry heading is not named in a statement of responsibility or in the publication details), make a note giving the name of the person or body (see rule 7B6) or the title (see rule 7B4).

29B. Specific applications

29B1. Two or more persons or corporate bodies involved. If the following subrules and examples refer to only one person or body, and two or three persons or bodies are involved in the work that you are cataloguing, make added entries under the headings for each.

If four or more persons or bodies are involved in a particular instance, make an added entry under the heading for the one named first in the chief source of information of the bibliographic resource being catalogued.

29B2. Examples of added entries. Typical examples of name added entries are:

a) collaborators

> The basement tapes / Bob Dylan & the Band
> (*songs written and performed by Dylan and the rock group the Band*)
> *Main entry under the heading for Dylan*
> *Added entry under the heading for the Band*

> Captions courageous, or, Comments from the gallery / by Bob Reisner and Hal Kapplow
> *Main entry under the heading for Reisner*
> *Added entry under the heading for Kapplow*

> What I think : weekly column / by R.H. Wheatley and/or Lila Hoffman-Thome
> (*an online resource*)
> *Main entry under the heading for Wheatley*
> *Added entry under the heading for Hoffman-Thome*

> Banned books 287 B.C. to 1978 A.D. ... / by Anne Lyon Haight ; updated and enlarged by Chandler B. Grannis
> *Main entry under the heading for Haight*
> *Added entry under the heading for Grannis*

> The Oxford book of wild flowers / illustrations by B.E. Nicholson ; text by S. Ary & M. Gregory
> *Main entry under the heading for Nicholson*
> *Added entries under the headings for Ary and Gregory*

Roman and pre-Roman glass in the Royal
Ontario Museum : a catalogue / John W.
Hayes
Main entry under the heading for the Museum (see rule 23B2)
Added entry under the heading for Hayes

b) editors, compilers, revisers, etc.

The Penguin book of animal verse /
introduced and edited by George MacBeth
Main entry under title
Added entry under the heading for MacBeth

Views of the Solar System / compiled
and maintained by Calvin J. Hamilton
    (*an online archive of photographs, data, text, graphics,*
    and videos)
Main entry under title
Added entry under the heading for Hamilton

The novels of Jane Austen / the text
based on collation of the early editions
by G.W. Chapman
Main entry under the heading for Austen
Added entry under the heading for Chapman

c) original authors

Hoyle's rules of games ... / edited
by Albert H. Morehead and Geoffrey
Mott-Smith
Main entry under the heading for Morehead
Added entry (name/title; see rule 29B4) under the heading
   for Hoyle
Added entry under the heading for Mott-Smith

The new Roget's thesaurus of the
English language in dictionary form / by
Norman Lewis
Main entry under the heading for Lewis
Added entry (name/title; see rule 29B4) under the heading
   for Roget

d) performers

> James Galway plays Mozart
> (*accompanied by the London Symphony Orchestra*)
> *Main entry under the heading for Mozart*
> *Added entries under the headings for Galway and the Orchestra*

> To Lefty from Willie
> (*sound recording of Lefty Frizzell's songs performed by Willie Nelson*)
> *Main entry under the heading for Frizzell*
> *Added entry under the heading for Nelson*

e) corporate bodies with responsibility beyond that of publishing.

> A field guide to the birds ... / text and illustrations by Roger Tory Peterson. -- 2nd rev. and enl. ed. / sponsored by the National Audubon Society
> *Main entry under the heading for Peterson*
> *Added entry under the heading for the Society*

> Desalination: a tape/slide presentation / Creative Media, Inc. for the Desalination Company
> *Main entry under title*
> *Added entries under the headings for the two companies*

> Fifty years of modern art, 1916-1966 / Edward B. Henning. -- Cleveland : Cleveland Museum of Art
> (*catalogue of a loan exhibition*)
> *Main entry under the heading for Henning*
> *Added entry under the heading for the Museum*

> Sex and the Californian / Present Topics, Inc.
> (*a videorecording*)
> *Main entry under title*
> *Added entry under the heading for Present Topics*

```
The bird web / maintained by Paul Doyle
at the Conoco Natural History Centre
```
   (*an online resource*)
Main entry under title
Added entries under the headings for Doyle and for the Centre

```
The Paris Commune of 1871 / by Frank
Jellinek
```
   (*a "Left Book Club edition"*)
Main entry under the heading for Jellinek
Added entry under the heading for the Club

```
Closing the catalog: proceedings of the
1978 and 1979 Library and Information
Technology Association institutes
```
Main entry under title
Added entry under the heading for the Association

```
Hampstead past and present / issued
with the approval of the Hampstead
Borough Council
```
Main entry under title
Added entry under the heading for the Council

29B3. Other related persons or bodies. If the heading will provide an important access point, make an added entry under the heading for any person or body that has a relationship to a work not covered in rules 23–28 or in the preceding parts of rule 29.

```
A short title catalogue of the Warren N.
and Suzanne B. Cordell collection of
dictionaries
```
   (*catalogue of a special collection held by the*
   Cunningham Library, Indiana State University)
Main entry under the heading for the Library
Added entries under the headings for W.N. and S.B. Cordell

```
Currents in anthropology : essays in
honor of Sol Tax / edited by Robert
Hinshaw
```
Main entry under title
Added entries under the headings for Tax and Hinshaw

29B4. Related works. Make an added entry under the main entry heading for a work to which the work being catalogued is closely related (see rules 26C, 27, and 28 for guidance in specific cases).

Make such entries in the form of the heading for the person or corporate body or title under which the related work is, or would be, entered. If the heading is for a person or corporate body, *and* the title of the related work differs from the title of the work being catalogued, add the title of the related work to the heading to form a name/title added entry heading.

> Gore Vidal's Caligula : a novel based on Gore Vidal's original screenplay / by William Howard
> *Main entry under the heading for Howard*
> *Added entry under the heading for the motion picture* Caligula
> *Added entry (name/title) under the heading for Vidal*

> The long riders : original motion picture sound track / music composed and arranged by Ry Cooder
> *Main entry under the heading for Cooder*
> *Added entry under the heading for the motion picture* The
>   long riders

If appropriate, substitute a uniform title (see rules 57–61) for a title proper in a name/title or title added entry heading.

> Adventures of Tom Sawyer / by Mark Twain ; rewritten for young readers by Felix Sutton
> *Main entry under the heading for Sutton*
> *Added entry (name/title) under the heading for Twain*
>   *followed by the uniform title* Tom Sawyer

29B5. Titles. Make an added entry under the title proper of every item entered under a personal heading, a corporate heading, or a uniform title.

Make an added entry also for any other title (cover title, caption title, running title, etc.) if it is significantly different from the title proper.

> Dental model / H.J. Brandon
>   (*title on container:* Elementary dental work)
> *Main entry under the heading for Brandon*
> *Added entries under title proper and* Elementary dental work

29B6. Special rules for translators and illustrators

a) *Translators.* If the main entry is under the heading for a corporate body *or* under a title, make an added entry under the heading for a translator.

> Proceedings of the 6th Annual Conference of Italian School Administrators / translated by L. Del Vecchio
> *Main entry under the heading for the Conference*
> *Added entry under the heading for Del Vecchio*

> The New Testament ... : a translation ... / by Ronald A. Knox
> *Main entry under the heading for the* New Testament
> *Added entry under the heading for Knox*

If the main entry is under the heading for a person, make an added entry under the heading for the translator if:

i) the translation is in verse

> The sonnets of Michelangelo / translated by Elizabeth Jennings
> *Main entry under the heading for Michelangelo*
> *Added entry under the heading for Jennings*

or ii) the work has been translated into the same language more than once

> The betrothed (I promessi sposi): a Milanese story of the seventeenth century / by Alessandro Manzoni ; translated by Daniel J. O'Connor
> (*one of a number of English translations of* I promessi sposi)
> *Main entry under the heading for Manzoni*
> *Added entry under the heading for O'Connor*

or iii) the wording of the chief source of information implies that the translator is the author.

> Thumbelina / Anne Smythe
> (*a translation of H.C. Andersen's* Tommelise)

Main entry under the heading for Andersen
Added entry under the heading for Smythe

b) *Illustrators.* Make an added entry under the heading for an illustrator if:

  i) in the chief source of information, the illustrator's name is given equal prominence with, or more prominence than, the name of the person or body used in the main entry heading

```
Insects : a guide to familiar American
insects / by Herbert S. Zim and Clarence
Cottam ; illustrated by James Gordon
Irving
```
      (all names given on the title page in the same size of type)
Main entry under the heading for Zim
Added entries under the headings for Cottam and Irving

or ii) the illustrations occupy half or more of the bibliographic resource

```
Hans Christian Andersen's The
nightingale / designed and illustrated
by Nancy Ekholm Burkert
```
      (Burkert's name not given equal prominence; the illustrations occupy more than half of the volume)
Main entry under the heading for Andersen
Added entry under the heading for Burkert

or iii) the illustrations are considered to be an important part of the work.

```
Handley Cross / by the author of Mr.
Sponge's sporting tour ; with seventeen
coloured illustrations and one hundred
woodcuts by John Leech
```
      (Leech's name not given equal prominence; most of the book is text; Leech is one of the most famous Victorian book illustrators)
Main entry under the heading for the author (Surtees)
Added entry under the heading for Leech

29B7. Series. Make an added entry under the heading for a series for each separately catalogued bibliographic resource in the series *if* the added entry provides a useful grouping of entries. *Optionally,* add the numeric or other designation of each work in the series.

```
The natural history of Selborne /
Gilbert White ... (The world's classics ;
no. 22)
```
Main entry under the heading for White
Added entry under: World's classics *or* World's classics ;
   no. 22

```
Piano concerto no. 2 in B flat, op. 83
/ Brahms ... (Family library of great
music ; album 4)
```
Main entry under the heading for Brahms
Added entry under: Family library of great music *or* Family
   library of great music ; album 4

```
Kitagawa Utamaro (1753-1806) / text by
Ichitaro Kondo ; English adaptation by
Charles S. Terry ... (Library of Japanese
art ; no. 5)
```
Main entry under the heading for Kondo
Added entry under: Library of Japanese art *or* Library of
   Japanese art ; no. 5

```
The golden key / by George MacDonald ;
with pictures by Maurice Sendak ... (A
yearling book)
```
Main entry under the heading for MacDonald
Added entry under: Yearling books

```
International distribution of catalogue
cards : present situation and future
prospects / R.S. Giljarevskij ... (Unesco
manuals for libraries ; 15)
```
Main entry under the heading for Giljarevskij
Added entry under: Unesco manuals for libraries *or* Unesco
   manuals for libraries ; 15

```
Books do furnish a room : a novel /
Anthony Powell ... (The music of time /
Anthony Powell ; 10)
```
Main entry under the heading for Powell
Added entry under: Powell, Anthony. Music of time *or*
    Powell, Anthony. Music of time ; 10

29B8. Analytical added entries. An analytical entry is an entry for:

a separately titled section of a work
or
a separate work contained in a collection.

Make analytical entries as required by your library's policy.
Two methods of making analytical entries are given here. Choose
the more appropriate for the item that you are cataloguing.

a) *Name/title added entry headings.* Make an analytical entry by
using the name/title or title heading of the part as an added
entry heading.

```
Melville, Herman
  Billy Budd
  Great short novels : an anthology /
by Edward Weeks. -- New York :
Literary Guild of America, c1941
  999 p. ; 26 cm.
  Contains twelve short novels by
English and American writers
```

b) *"In"* entries. If you require more detail in the analytical entry,
make an "In" entry. Such entries consist of:

For the part
        the name/title *or* title heading

        the title proper and statement(s) of responsibility (see
           rule 1)

and, if relevant,
        the edition statement (see rule 2)

        the publication, etc., details (see rule 4)

the extent, other physical details, dimensions (see rule 5)

notes (see rule 7)

the word *In*

and, *for the whole item*

    the name/title *or* title heading

    the title proper and statement(s) of responsibility (see
      rule 1)

and, if relevant,

    the edition statement (see rule 2)

    the publication, etc., details (see rule 4).

```
Eliot, George
   The lifted veil / George Eliot. --
p. 198-246 ; 26 cm.
   In Eliot, George. Silas Marner ; The
lifted veil ; Brother Jacob. -- London :
Oxford University Press, 1906

Dickens, Charles
   A Christmas carol / by Charles
Dickens. -- p. 171-234 : ill. (some
col.) ; 24 cm.
   In Once upon a time : the fairy tale
world of Arthur Rackham. -- London :
Heinemann, 1972

Tolkien, J.R.R.
   Guide to the names in the Lord of
the rings / J.R.R. Tolkien. -- p. 168-
216 ; 20 cm.
   In A Tolkien compass / edited by
Jared Lobdell. -- New York :
Ballantine, 1980
```

Headings for Persons

Contents

Additions to Personal Names

Additions to Distinguish Identical Names

30. INTRODUCTION

In making a heading for a person, take the following three steps.

First, choose the name that will be the basis for the heading. Most persons are only known by one name. In some cases, however, a person is identified by two or more names *or* by two or more forms of the same name. For example, the same woman is known as *Jacqueline Kennedy* and *Jacqueline Onassis,* and the same man is known as *Herblock* and *Herbert Block.*

Second, decide which part of the chosen name should be the first word in the heading (the "filing element"). Again, in the majority of cases this is simply the surname.[1] In some cases, however, the choice is not so obvious. For example, should it be *Gaulle, Charles de* or *De Gaulle, Charles?*

Third, make references from different names for the same person or from different parts of the chosen name. For example, you should refer from *Geisel, Theodore* to *Seuss, Dr.*; from *Clay, Cassius* to *Ali, Muhammad*; and from *Da Vinci, Leonardo* and *Vinci, Leonardo da* to *Leonardo, da Vinci.*

Rules 31–44 deal with the first two steps and with their associated problems. Rule 63 deals with the third.

---

1. "Surname," as used in these rules, includes any name used as a family name.

Choice of Name

31. GENERAL RULE

31A. Choose, as the basis for the heading, the name by which a person is commonly known. It may be the person's real name, pseudonym, nickname, title, name in religion, initials, or any other type of name. For persons using pseudonyms, see also rule 32A.

31B. Apply the following subrules to decide the form of name by which a person is commonly known.

31B1. Names containing surnames. If a person is identified by a name that contains a surname:

a) use the form of name that appears in the chief sources of information (see rule 0A) of manifestations of works by that person in his or her language

<pre>
        Clara Jones

        Willie Nelson

        Lester Del Rey

        Elinor M. Brent-Dyer

        Studs Terkel

        D.H. Lawrence
    not David Herbert Lawrence

        P.G. Wodehouse
    not Pelham Grenville Wodehouse
    not Pelham Wodehouse

        Morris West
            (form of name most commonly found in chief sources)
    not Morris L. West
            (form of name found occasionally)

        Bertrand Russell
    not Bertrand, third Earl Russell
</pre>

Sebastien Japrisot
(*pseudonym*)

not   Jean-Baptiste Rossi
(*real name*)

George Eliot
(*pseudonym*)

not   Mary Ann Evans
(*name before marriage*)

not   Mary Ann Cross
(*married name*)

Duke Ellington

not   Edward Kennedy Ellington

b) if the chief sources of information are of little or no help (as, for example, with painters, sculptors, and choreographers), *or* if the person is not primarily known as a creator of works (as, for example, with politicians and motion picture actors), use the form found in reference sources, other books, and articles issued in the person's language or country of residence or activity.

Ben Nicholson
(*painter*)

Aristide Maillol
(*sculptor*)

Okumura Masanobu
(*print maker*)

Kirk Douglas
(*film star*)

not   Issur Danielovitch Demsky
(*real name*)

Rita Hayworth
(*film star*)

not   Margarita Carmen Cansino
(*real name*)

Harry S. Truman

```
        Jimmy Carter
  not   James Earl Carter
```

31B2. Names not containing surnames. If a person is identified by a name that does not contain a surname:

a) use the name by which he or she is identified in English-language reference sources

```
        Pope John XXIII
  not   Joannes Papa XXIII

        Saint Francis
  not   San Francesco

        Confucius
  not   K'ung-tzu

        Horace
  not   Quintus Horatius Flaccus

        Alexander the Great
  not   Alexandros ho Megas

        Saint Joan of Arc
  not   Sainte Jeanne d'Arc

        White Antelope
          (Cheyenne chief)

        Queen Elizabeth II
```

b) if you cannot find the name in English-language reference sources available to you, use the form of name that appears in the chief sources of information (see rule 0A) of manifestations of works by that person in his or her language.

```
        A.E.
          (pseudonym)
  not   George William Russell
          (real name)

        Howling Wolf
          (blues singer)
```

```
LL Cool J
  (rapper)
```

```
Herblock
```
not   `Herbert Block`

```
Ximenes
  (crossword puzzle creator)
```
not   `Derek Macnutt`
          (*real name*)

31C. Include any titles of royalty or nobility (see also rule 40) that usually appear as part of the name.

```
Duchess of Windsor
```

```
Diana, Princess of Wales
```

```
Lady Jane Grey
```

31D. If the name contains a surname, omit terms (other than those of royalty or nobility, see rule 31C) that appear with the name.

```
Karen Schmidt
```
not   `Doctor Karen Schmidt`

```
Jane Lavelle
```
not   `Lieutenant Jane Lavelle`

If the name does not contain a surname *or* if it consists of only a surname and a word or phrase, include any terms that normally appear as part of the name.

```
Sister Mary Hilary
```

```
Thomas the Rhymer
```

```
Geoffrey of Monmouth
```

```
Brother Antoninus
```

```
Grandma Moses
```

```
Dr. Seuss
```

32. CHOICE BETWEEN DIFFERENT NAMES

32A. Persons using pseudonyms

32A1. One pseudonym. If all the works by a person appear under one pseudonym, choose the pseudonym. Make a reference (see rule 63A) from the real name if you know it.

> ```
>       Martin Ross
> not   Violet Frances Martin
> 
>       Henry Green
> not   Henry York
> 
>       Woody Allen
> not   Allen Stewart Konigsberg
> 
>       Bryher
> not   Anne Winifred Ellerman
> ```
>   (*name before marriage*)
> ```
> not   Anne Winifred McAlmon
> ```
>   (*married name*)
> ```
> not   Anne Winifred Macpherson
> ```
>   (*married name*)

If two or more collaborators use a single pseudonym, choose that pseudonym. Make references from the names of the collaborators if they are known.

> ```
>       Emma Lathen
> ```
>   (*pseudonym of Mary J. Latis and Martha Hennisart*)

32A2. More than one pseudonym. If a person uses more than one pseudonym *or* his or her real name and one or more pseudonym(s) *and* if the person has

> *either* established separate bibliographic identities (that is, has published groups of similar works under one name and groups of similar works under one or more other names)
>
> *or* is a contemporary author

choose, as the basis for the heading for each work, the name found in the chief sources of information of manifestations of that work. Make references (see rule 63B) to connect the names.

```
Lewis Carroll
Charles Lutwidge Dodgson
```
  (*separate bibliographic identities*)

```
Rampling, Anne
Rice, Anne
Roquelaure, A.M.
```
  (*pseudonyms used by the same person*)

```
Molly Keane
```
  (*real name used in some works*)
```
M.J. Farrell
```
  (*pseudonym used in some works*)

```
Denys Watkins-Pitchford
```
  (*real name used in some works*)
```
BB
```
  (*pseudonym used in some works*)

```
Gore Vidal
```
  (*real name used in most works*)
```
Edgar Box
```
  (*pseudonym used in some works*)

If different names for such a person appear in different editions of the same work *or* if two or more names appear in the same edition, choose (in this order of preference):

  the name that has most frequently appeared in editions
    of the work

  the name appearing in the latest edition of the work.

```
Terror by day / by John Creasey
writing as Gordon Ashe
```
  (*all previous editions published as:* by Gordon Ashe)
  Choose **Gordon Ashe** *as the basis for the heading for this work*

```
Belinda / Anne Rice writing as Anne
Rampling
```
  (*one earlier edition published as:* by Anne Rampling)
  Choose **Anne Rice** *as the basis for the heading for this work*

If a person using more than one pseudonym *or* his or her real name and one or more pseudonym(s):

> *neither* has established separate bibliographic identities

> *nor* is a contemporary author

choose the name by which that person has come to be identified in later editions of manifestations of his or her works, in critical works, and/or in reference sources.

```
        William Thackeray
  not   Michael Angelo Titmarsh
  not   Mr. Yellowplush
```

32B. Persons not using pseudonyms

If a person, other than one using one or more pseudonyms (see rule 32A), is known by more than one name *or* more than one form of a name, choose the name or form of name (if there is one) by which the person is clearly most commonly known (see rule 31B).

Otherwise, choose (in this order of preference):

1) the name that appears most frequently in manifestations of the person's works
2) the name that appears most frequently in current reference sources
3) the latest name.

```
        Gerald R. Ford
  not   Gerald R. Gardner
  not   Leslie King
          (earlier names)

        Bob Hope
  not   Leslie Townes Hope

        Jacqueline Onassis
  not   Jacqueline Bouvier
  not   Jacqueline Kennedy
          (earlier names)

        W.H. Auden
  not   Wystan Hugh Auden
```

```
        Tony  Benn
not     Anthony  Wedgewood  Benn
            (fuller form)
not     Lord  Stansgate
            (disclaimed peerage)

        Muhammad  Ali
not     Cassius  Clay
            (earlier name)

        Alicia  Markova
not     Alice  Marks
            (earlier name)

        Anton  Dolin
not     Patrick  Healey-Kay
            (earlier name)
```

Entry Element

33. GENERAL RULE

If a person's name (chosen in accordance with rules 31 and 32) consists of more than one part, choose one of the parts as the entry element (the part under which the heading is filed and/or by which it is retrieved). Choose the entry element by following rules 34–39.

33A. Order of elements

33A1. If the entry element is the first part of the name, enter the name in direct order.

```
        Ram  Gopal

        Mobutu  Sese  Seko
```

33A2. If the entry element is not the first part of the name, transfer the parts that precede it to follow the entry element. Follow the entry element by a comma (,).

```
        Ronstadt,  Linda
            (name: Linda Ronstadt)
```

```
Procter, Adelaide Ann
```
(*name:* Adelaide Ann Procter)

```
Griffith-Joyner, Florence
```
(*name:* Florence Griffith-Joyner)

33A3. If the entry element is the proper name in a title of nobility, see rule 35.

```
Winchilsea, Anne Finch, Countess of
```
(*name:* Anne Finch, Countess of Winchilsea)

34. ENTRY UNDER SURNAME

34A. General rule

Enter a name containing a surname or consisting of a surname under the surname unless the name is to be entered under a title of nobility (see rule 35).

```
Fonda, Jane

Harris, Emmy-Lou

Gorman, R.C.

Waters, Muddy

Mantovani
```

34B. Part of the name treated as a surname

If the name does not contain a surname but contains an element that identifies the person and functions as a surname, enter under that element.

```
X, Laura
```

34C. Compound surnames

34C1. Preliminary rule. Apply the following subrules to names that contain, or appear to contain, compound surnames (those consisting of two or more proper names). Apply the subrules in the order in which they appear.

34C2. Hyphenated surnames. If the parts of the compound surname are usually or sometimes hyphenated, enter under the first element of the compound surname.

> Williams-Ellis, Amabel
>
> Ffrangcon-Davis, Gwen

34C3. Unhyphenated surnames. Some married women. Apply this rule to the names of married women with unhyphenated surnames consisting of the surname before marriage and the husband's surname.

Enter under the first element of the surname if the woman's language is Czech, French, Hungarian, Italian, or Spanish.

> Bonacci Brunamonti, Alinda
> (*Italian*)

Enter under the husband's surname if the woman's language is other than those listed above.

> Wilder, Laura Ingalls
> (*American, English speaker*)
>
> Larsson, Inger Olson
> (*Swedish*)

34C4. Unhyphenated surnames. Others. Enter under the first element of the compound surname unless the person's language is Portuguese.

> Johnson Smith, Geoffrey
>
> Strauss und Torney, Lulu

but

> Silva, Ovidio Saraiva de Carvalho e
> (*Portuguese*)

34C5. Nature of surname uncertain. If the name appears to contain a compound surname but you are not sure:

a) enter under the last part of the name if the person's language is English or one of the Scandinavian languages

> Robertson, E. Arnot
>
> Jenkins, Florence Foster

b) enter under the first part of the apparent compound surname if the person's language is neither English nor one of the Scandinavian languages.

```
Gonzalez Valdés, Selene
```

34D. Surnames with separately written prefixes

34D1. Articles and prepositions. If the surname includes an article (for example, "le") *or* a preposition (for example, "van") or a combination of the two (for example, "de la," "della"), enter under the part of the surname that is most commonly used as the entry element in listings in the person's language or country of residence. See the list of languages and language groups below. For languages not included in this list, see the full *AACR2*.

If a person has used two or more languages, enter the name according to (in order of preference):

a) the rule for the language of most of his or her works
b) the rule for English (if English is one of the languages)
c) the rule for the language of the country of his or her residence
d) the rule for the language of the name.

Languages and language groups

ENGLISH. Enter under the prefix.

```
De Mornay, Rebecca

De la Rue, Elaine

L'Amour, Louis

Le Gallienne, Eva

Du Bois, Cora Alice

Van Alstyne, Carol

Von Braun, Wernher
```

FRENCH. If the prefix consists of an article (for example, "le") or of a contraction of an article and a preposition (for example, "du"), enter under the prefix.

```
Le Bordays, Christiane

Du Guillet, Pernette

Des Rosiers, Rachel
```

Otherwise enter under the part of the name following the preposition.

```
Graffigny, Françoise de

La Bois, Ghislaine de
```

GERMAN. If the prefix consists of an article or of a contraction of an article and a preposition (for example, "Vom"), enter under the prefix.

```
Am Ende, Eva

Zum Wald-Mertens, Wera
```

Otherwise enter under the part of the name following the prefix.

```
Goethe, Johann Wolfgang von

Beethoven, Ludwig van
```

ITALIAN. Enter a modern name under the prefix.

```
D'Amato, Nicola

Da Caprile, Nello

Dell'Arte, Antonietta
```

For mediaeval and early modern names, see the full *AACR2*.

SPANISH. If the prefix consists of an article only, enter under it.

```
Las Heras, Elvira
```

Enter all other names under the part following the prefix.

```
Casas, Bartolomé de las
```

34D2. Other prefixes. If the prefix is not an article, *or* preposition, *or* a combination of the two, enter under the prefix.

```
Abu Jaber, Kamel

Ap Rhys, Angharad
```

```
Ben Gurion, David

O'Casey, Sean

FitzGerald, Mary

Ní Chuilleanáin, Eiléan
```

35. ENTRY UNDER TITLE OF NOBILITY

35A. Definition

A person of modern times identified by a title of nobility has a name that consists of:

> forename(s)—for example: Anne; George Gordon
>
> surname—for example: Finch; Byron
>
> title—for example: Countess of Winchilsea; Baron Byron

Consider those persons who *either* use their titles rather than their surnames in manifestations of their works *or* are listed under their titles in reference sources[2] to be commonly identified by their titles.

35B. General rule

If a person is commonly identified by a title, enter under the proper name in his or her title of nobility. Follow the proper name by the person's forename(s) and surname (in that order) and by the term of rank[3] in the person's language.

```
Byron, George Gordon Byron, Baron
```
> (*name appears in his works as:* Lord Byron)

```
Nairne, Carolina Nairne, Baroness
```
> (*name appears in her works as:* Baroness Nairne *or* Lady Nairne)

---

2. Disregard reference sources that list members of the nobility *either* all under title *or* all under surname.

3. The terms of rank in the United Kingdom peerage are Duke, Duchess, Marquess (Marquis), Marchioness, Earl, Countess, Viscount, Viscountess, Baron, and Baroness.

> Pompadour, Antoinette Poisson, marquise de
> (*name appears in reference works as*: Madame de
> Pompadour)

> Russell of Liverpool, Edward Frederick
> Langley Russell, Baron
> (*name appears in his works as*: Lord Russell of
> Liverpool)

Enter a person with a title who is not commonly identified by his or her title under surname (see rules 34 and 40) *or* given name (see rules 36 and 40) as appropriate.

35C. If a person acquires a title of nobility, gives up such a title, or acquires a new title of nobility, follow the instructions in rule 32B in choosing the name to be used as the basis for the heading.

> Caradon, Hugh Foot, Baron
> (*previously* Hugh Foot)

> Benn, Tony
> (*previously* Viscount Stansgate; *title given up*)

36. ENTRY UNDER GIVEN NAME, ETC.

Enter a person with a name that does not include a surname *and* who is not commonly identified by a title of nobility under the part of the name under which the person is listed in reference sources. Include in the heading any words or phrases that are usually associated with the name. Precede such words or phrases by a comma (,).

> Bryher
>
> Emma, of Rheims
>
> John, the Baptist
>
> White Antelope, Cheyenne chief
>
> Leonardo, da Vinci
>
> Teresa, of Avila, Saint
>
> Mary, Queen of Scots

```
Mary II, Queen of England and Wales

Margaret, Princess, Countess of Snowdon

John XXIII, Pope
```

37. ENTRY OF ROMAN NAMES

Enter a Roman of classical times (before 476 of the Common Era) under the part of the name most commonly used as entry element in modern reference sources.

```
Messalina, Valeria

Cicero, Marcus Tullius
```

38. ENTRY UNDER INITIALS, LETTERS, OR NUMERALS

Enter in direct order a name consisting of initials, letters, or numerals.

```
BB

H.D.

110908
```

39. ENTRY UNDER PHRASE

39A. Enter in direct order a name that consists of a phrase that does not include a forename (see rule 36).

```
Dr. X

Father Time
```

Enter in direct order a name that consists of a forename *and* a word or phrase that is *neither* a title (for example, "Lady") *nor* a term of address (for example, "Aunt").

```
Boy George
```

39B. If a name consists of a phrase that contains a surname, enter under the surname.

> Moses, Grandma

If a name consists of a forename and *either* a title *or* a term of address, enter under the forename.

> Pierre, Chef

> Emma, Aunt

Additions to Personal Names

40. TITLES OF NOBILITY

In the case of the name of a nobleman or noblewoman not entered under title (see rule 35), add the title of nobility in the person's language *if* the title or part of the title commonly appears with the name in works by the person or in reference sources.[4] In case of doubt, omit the title.

> Orczy, Emmuska, Baroness

but

> Buchan, John
> (*title* Baron Tweedsmuir *not used in most works*)

41. ADDITIONS TO NAMES THAT DO NOT APPEAR TO BE NAMES

If the name by which a person is identified does not appear to be the name of a person, add a suitable English designation in parentheses.

> Taj Mahal (Musician)

> Madonna (Singer/actress)

---

4. Disregard reference sources dealing only with the nobility and gentry.

Additions to Distinguish Identical Names

42. ADDITIONS TO NAMES CONTAINING, OR CONSISTING OF, INITIALS

If the name by which a person is identified contains, or consists of, initials *and* the fuller form is known, add the spelled-out form (in parentheses) if necessary to distinguish between names that are otherwise identical.

```
Smith, Joan E. (Joan Elaine)

Smith, Joan E. (Joan Eleanor)

K.M. (Kate Maclellan)

K.M. (Karen Morgan)
```

43. DATES

Add the years of birth and/or death as the last element of a heading if the heading is otherwise identical to another. Give the dates in the form shown below.

```
Smith, Joan, 1924-
    (living person)

Smith, Joan, 1837-1896
    (both dates known)

Smith, Joan, 1837?-1896
    (year of birth probably 1837)

Smith, Joan, b. 1825
    (year of death unknown)

Smith, Joan, d. 1859
    (year of birth unknown)

Smith, Joan E. (Joan Elaine), 1894-1957

Smith, Joan E. (Joan Elaine), 1941-
```

44. If *neither* a fuller form of name *nor* dates are available, do not add anything and interfile the headings.

```
Andrew, Janet
   Constructing balsa-wood models ...
1956

Andrew, Janet
   She was only a gentleman's toy ...
1904

Andrew, Janet
   A story of the Indian jungles ...
1857
```

Geographic Names

Contents

45. INTRODUCTION

The names of places are used:

a) to distinguish between corporate bodies with the same name

```
Labour Party (Ireland)

Labour Party (New Zealand)
```

b) as additions to other corporate names (for example, conferences)

```
Conference on the Problems of the
    Rain Forest (1988 : San Francisco,
    Calif.)
```

c) often, as headings for governments.

```
Denmark

California

Tyne and Wear

Chicago
```

46. GENERAL RULE

46A. Choice of name

Give the name of a place in the form found in (in this order of preference):

1) current English-language gazetteers and atlases
2) other current English-language reference sources.

```
          Denmark
    not   Danmark

          Vienna
    not   Wien

          Mexico City
    not   Ciudad de México

          Switzerland
    not   Helvetia
    not   Schweiz
    not   Suisse
    not   Svizzera

          Rio de Janeiro

          Ciudad Juárez

          Amsterdam

          Sri Lanka
```

46B. Additions to geographic names

46B1. No addition. Do not add the name of a larger place to the name of a country

```
          Andorra
    not   Andorra (Europe)

          Peru
    not   Peru (South America)
```

or a state, province, territory, etc., of Australia, Canada, Malaysia, or the U.S.

```
        British Columbia
  not   British Columbia (Canada)

        Nevada
  not   Nevada (U.S.)
```

or any of the following parts of the British Isles: England, the Republic of Ireland, Northern Ireland, Scotland, Wales, the Isle of Man, the Channel Islands.

46B2. Addition. Add to the name of a place, other than one of those listed above, the name of the appropriate larger place in which it is located. Use standard abbreviations for the names of the larger places.

If the place name is being used as an entry element, make the addition in parentheses.

```
        Birmingham (Ala.)

        Birmingham (England)
```

If the place name is being used as an addition, precede the larger place by a comma.

```
        Regents College (London, England)

        Conference on Knowledge Science (1987 :
            Chicago, Ill.)
```

Examples of appropriate additions are:

Cities
```
        Hyde Park (Chicago, Ill.)
```

States, territories, provinces, etc.
```
        Newcastle (N.S.W.)

        Vancouver (B.C.)

        Vancouver (Wash.)

        Paris (Ill.)

        Urbana (Ill.)

        Urbana (Ohio)
```

Parts of the British Isles

```
Dorset (England)

Glasgow (Scotland)

Bangor (Wales)

Bangor (Northern Ireland)

Waterville (Ireland)
```

Countries

```
Formosa (Argentina)

Lucca (Italy)

Odense (Denmark)

Paris (France)

Kiev (Ukraine)
```

47. CHANGES OF NAME

If the name of the place changes, use the latest name

```
      Namibia
not   South-West Africa

      Congo
not   Zaïre
```

unless you are referring to the place at a time when it used the earlier name. For example, use "Gold Coast" if you are referring to the place before March 6, 1957, and "Ghana" for the place since that date.

Headings for Corporate Bodies

Contents

Subordinate Bodies

48. INTRODUCTION

In making a heading for a corporate body, take as many of the following five steps as are applicable.

First, choose the name that will be the basis for the heading.

Most bodies are known by only one name. In some cases, however, a body is identified by two or more names (see rules 49–50).

Second, decide whether the name needs an addition to distinguish it from other names (see rule 51).

Third, if the body is a conference, other meeting, exhibition, fair, etc., make the omissions and additions set out in rule 52.

Fourth, if the body is part of another body or is an agency of government, decide whether the body is to be entered directly or subordinately (see rules 53–56).

Fifth, make references from different names for the same body or from different parts of the chosen name (see rule 64).

49. GENERAL RULE

49A. Form of heading

Decide the form of name of a corporate body (see rule 23B1) from (in this order of preference):

1) bibliographic resources issued by the body in its language
2) reference sources (including books and articles about the body).

If the name contains (*or* consists of) initials, omit or include full stops according to the predominant usage of the body.

49B. Direct or indirect entry

Enter a corporate body directly under its own name *unless* rule 54 provides for entering it under the name of a higher or related body *or* rule 55 provides for entering it under the name of a government.

```
A-400 Group

American Library Association

California State University, Fresno

Church of England

Cleveland Orchestra

Cowboy Junkies
  (musical group)

F.W. Woolworth Company

George Fry & Associates

International Wildlife Conference ...⁵

Juilliard Quartet

Microsoft

Museum of Modern Art

Oral Roberts University

Royal Automobile Club

Scripture Union

Twentieth Century-Fox

University of Iowa

Valley of Peace Lutheran Church
```

49C. Changes of name

If the name of a corporate body has changed, establish a new heading under the new name for works appearing under that name. Refer from the old heading to the new and from the new heading to the old.

```
Ohio College Library Center
  see also the later heading: OCLC
```

---

5. For additions to the names of conferences, see rule 52C.

```
OCLC
     see also the earlier heading: Ohio
     College Library Center
```

50. VARIANT NAMES

50A. Language

If the body's name appears in different languages, use the form in the official language of the body.

```
            Société historique franco-américaine
     not    Franco-American Historical Society
```

If there is no official English form, use:

> *either* the form in a language familiar to the users of your catalogue
>
> *or,* if the body's name is in a language unfamiliar to the users of your catalogue, a documented translation of the name into English.

```
            Japan Productivity Centre
     not    Nihon Seisansei Hombu
```

50B. Governments

Use the conventional English name of a government[6] as the heading. The conventional name is the geographic name (see rules 45–47) of the area over which the government has jurisdiction.

```
            France
     not    République française

            Sweden
     not    Konungariket Sverige
```

---

6. "Government," as used in these rules, means any body (national, federal, regional, or local) that has jurisdiction over a particular area: country, state, province, county, city, municipality, etc.

```
            Puerto Rico
    not     Commonwealth of Puerto Rico

            Dorset
    not     County of Dorset

            Rhode Island
    not     State of Rhode Island and Providence
            Plantations
```

50C. Other variant names

50C1. If, in the same period of time, a body uses different names in bibliographic resources issued by it, use the name that appears in chief sources of information (see rule 0A) rather than forms found elsewhere.

50C2. If different forms appear in the chief sources of information, use (in this order of preference):

a) the form not linked to other words in the chief source

```
            Champaign County Museum
    not     County Museum
```
>   (*appears as* County Museum *in book titles, for*
>   *example,* Victorian furniture in the County Museum)

b) the predominant form

```
            Pierpont Morgan Library
```
>   (*predominant form*)
```
    not     Morgan Library
```
>   (*occasional form*)

```
            Association of College and Research
            Libraries
```
>   (*predominant form*)
```
    not     ACRL
```
>   (*occasional form*)

c) the brief form

```
            AFAS
    not     Air Force Aid Society
```

```
        AFL-CIO
not     American Federation of Labor and
            Congress of Industrial Organizations

        Unesco
not     United Nations Educational, Scientific,
            and Cultural Organization
```

d) the later or latest form.

```
        Hendon Natural History Association
not     Hendon Naturalists Association
```
         (*two items issued; the first under* Hendon Naturalists
         Association, *the second under* Hendon Natural History
         Association)

51. ADDITIONS TO CORPORATE NAMES

51A. General rule

If two or more bodies have the same name, make additions in parentheses as instructed below. Use standard abbreviations for the names of larger places added to place names.

51B. Names of countries, states, etc.

If the body is identified with a country, state, province, etc., rather than with a local place, add the name of that country, state, province, etc.

```
        National Portrait Gallery (United Kingdom)

        National Portrait Gallery (U.S.)

        Republican Party (Ill.)

        Republican Party (Mo.)
```

51C. In the case of all other bodies, add, as appropriate:

the name of the local place in which the body is located

```
        Roosevelt Junior High School (Eugene, Ore.)

        Roosevelt Junior High School (Fresno, Calif.)
```

```
Royal Hospital (Chelsea, London)

Royal Hospital (Victoria, B.C.)

United Methodist Church (Urbana, Ill.)

United Methodist Church (Urbana, Ohio)
```

or the name of the institution in which the body is located

```
Newman Club (Brooklyn College)

Newman Club (University of Maryland)
```

or the year of founding or the years of the body's existence

```
Scientific Society of San Antonio
  (1892-1894)

Scientific Society of San Antonio
  (1904-  )
```

or any other appropriate word or phrase in English.

```
Church of God (Adventist)

Church of God (Apostolic)

Congo (Democratic Republic)

Congo (Brazzaville)

St. James' Church (Manhattan, New York,
  N.Y. : Catholic)

St. James' Church (Manhattan, New York,
  N.Y. : Episcopal)
```

52. CONFERENCES, CONGRESSES, MEETINGS, ETC.

52A. General rule

Give the name of a conference as it appears in chief sources of information. If different forms of the name of the same conference appear in chief sources of information, see rule 50.

52B. Omissions

Omit words that denote the number, frequency, or year of the conference.

> Symposium on the Pre-Raphaelites
>
> *not* Annual Symposium on the Pre-Raphaelites

> Conference on Co-ordination of Galactic
> Research
>
> *not* Second Conference on Co-ordination of
> Galactic Research

> Workshop on Cataloguing Rules and
> Principles
>
> *not* 1987 Workshop on Cataloguing Rules and
> Principles

52C. Additions to individual conference names

Add to the heading for an individual conference:

> its number (if there is one)
>
> the year in which it was held
>
> the location (city or institution) in which it was held.

> Conference on the Central Nervous
> System and Behavior (2nd : 1959 :
> Princeton University)

> Conference on Solid Earth Problems
> (1970 : Buenos Aires, Argentina)

> Colloquium on Law and Ethics (1987 :
> University of Chicago)

> Conference on Third World Debt (2nd :
> 1988 : Cambridge, Mass.)

> Clinic on Library Applications of Data
> Processing (13th : 1976 : Urbana,
> Ill.)

52D. Series of conferences

If the heading is for a number of conferences, do not add the number, date, or location to the heading.

> Symposia on Old Growth Forests

Subordinate Bodies

53. SUBORDINATE BODIES ENTERED DIRECTLY

Enter a subordinate body[7] (including a body created or controlled by a government) directly under its own name *unless* it does not have an individualizing name (see rule 54) *or* it is a government agency to be entered under the name of the government (see rule 55).

> Henry Madden Library
> *not* California State University, Fresno.
> Henry Madden Library
>
> Harvard Medical School
> *not* Harvard University. Medical School
>
> Illini Union
> *not* University of Illinois at Urbana-
> Champaign. Illini Union
>
> Library and Information Technology
> Association
> *not* American Library Association. Library
> and Information Technology
> Association
>
> Symposium on Protein Metabolism ...
> *not* Nutrition Symposium. Symposium on
> Protein Metabolism

---

7. "Subordinate bodies," as used in these rules, include related bodies. A related body is one that, though not an administrative part of a higher body, is closely related to it. Examples of related bodies are: "friends" groups; staff associations; staff clubs.

```
       Humboldt State University
not    California State University. Humboldt
          Campus

       British Library
not    United Kingdom. British Library

       Amtrak
not    United States. Amtrak

       Canada Institute for Scientific and
          Technical Information
not    Canada. Institute for Scientific and
          Technical Information

       Exmoor National Park
not    United Kingdom. Exmoor National Park

       University of Montana
not    Montana. University

       Dundee Harbour Trust
not    United Kingdom. Dundee Harbour Trust
```

54. SUBORDINATE BODIES ENTERED SUBORDINATELY

Enter a subordinate body (other than a body created or controlled by a government, see rule 55) as a subheading of the higher body if:

the name of the subordinate body includes the whole name of the higher body

> American Legion. Auxiliary
> (*name:* American Legion Auxiliary)

> Friends of the Earth. Camden Friends
> of the Earth
> (*name:* Camden Friends of the Earth)

> OCLC. Illinois OCLC Users Group
> (*name:* Illinois OCLC Users Group)

University of Southampton. Mathematical
Society
(*name:* Mathematical Society of the University of
Southampton)

but

BBC Symphony Orchestra

not   British Broadcasting Corporation.
Symphony Orchestra

or the subordinate body has a name that is general in nature.

California State University, Fresno.
College of Arts and Humanities

International Council on Social
Welfare. Canadian Committee

Sondley Reference Library. Friends of
the Library

Arthur Wondley Corporation. Research
Division

California Home Economics Association.
Orange District

Dartmouth College. Class of 1980

In case of doubt, enter the body directly.

Human Resources Centre (London, England)

not   Tavistock Institute of Human Relations.
Human Resources Centre

55. GOVERNMENT AGENCIES ENTERED SUBORDINATELY

55A. General rule

Enter the name of a body created or controlled by a government under the heading for that government when it belongs to one or more of the following types.

TYPE 1. An agency with a name that is general in nature.

> Vermont. Department of Water Resources
>
> United States. Division of Wildlife Service
>
> Canada. Royal Commission on Banking and Finance
>
> Fresno County (Calif.). Board of Supervisors

In case of doubt, enter the body directly.

> National Portrait Gallery (United Kingdom)
>
> *not* United Kingdom. National Portrait Gallery

TYPE 2. An agency that has no other agency above it (for example, a ministry).

> Australia. Ministry of the Interior
>
> United Kingdom. Home Office
>
> United States. Department of State

TYPE 3. A legislative body (for example, a parliament, city council, or state legislature).

> United Kingdom. Parliament
>
> United States. Congress
>
> Virginia. General Assembly
>
> San Francisco (Calif.). Board of Supervisors

TYPE 4. A court.

> United States. Supreme Court
>
> United Kingdom. High Court of Justice

```
United States. District Court
  (Delaware)

Queensland. Supreme Court
```

TYPE 5. A major armed service (see also rule 56B).

```
Australia. Royal Australian Navy

United Kingdom. Army

United States. Marine Corps
```

TYPE 6. An embassy, consulate, etc.

```
Canada. Embassy (U.S.)

Canada. Embassy (Ireland)

Canada. Consulate (Los Angeles, Calif.)
```

55B. Government officials

Enter heads of state and other government officials who are not identified with the name of a particular agency as instructed below.

55B1. Sovereigns, presidents, heads of state, etc. Give the name of the government followed by the name of the office, the dates of incumbency, and the brief name of the person.

```
United Kingdom. Sovereign (1936-1952 :
  George VI)

United States. President (1993-2001 :
  Clinton)

California. Governor (1999-2003: Davis)
```

55B2. Other government officials. Give the name of the government followed by the name of the office.

```
Canada. Prime Minister

New Zealand. Governor-General

Philadelphia (Pa.). Mayor
```

56. DIRECT OR INDIRECT SUBORDINATE ENTRY

56A. General rule

If a subordinate body or government agency to be entered subordinately (see rules 54–55) is part of another subordinately entered body or agency, omit the intervening body or bodies *unless* the heading would not provide adequate identification without them.

> United States. Office of Human
>   Development Services
not United States. Department of Health,
>   Education, and Welfare. Office of
>   Human Development Services
but
> United Kingdom. Home Office. Personnel
>   Division
not United Kingdom. Personnel Division

56B. Armed services

If a government agency is part of a major armed service, enter it as a subheading of that major armed service.

> United Kingdom. Army. Middlesex
>   Regiment
>
> United States. Army. Corps of Engineers
>
> United Kingdom. Army. Infantry
>   Regiment, 57th
>
> United States. Navy. Torpedo Squadron 8

Uniform Titles

Contents

57. INTRODUCTION

57A. A uniform title is a title that brings together entries for two or more manifestations of the same work, when those manifestations have different titles proper. It is also used to identify a work when the title by which it is known is different from the title proper of the manifestation. Use of uniform titles is *optional,* and the need for them will vary from catalogue to catalogue and from work to work.

57B. If the entry is under a name heading, place the uniform title between the name heading and the title proper, and enclose the uniform title in square brackets.

```
        Shakespeare, William
          [Hamlet]
            Shakespeare's Hamlet
```

```
Shakespeare, William
  [Hamlet]
  The tragedy of Hamlet, Prince of
Denmark
```

If there is no name heading, give the uniform title as the heading.

```
Arabian nights
  The book of a thousand nights and a
night
```

```
Arabian nights
  Stories from the Arabian nights
```

57C. Omit an initial article from a uniform title.

```
     Dickens, Charles
       [Pickwick papers]
not  Dickens, Charles
       [The Pickwick papers]
```

```
     Hugo, Victor
       [Misérables]
not  Hugo, Victor
       [Les misérables]
```

58. GENERAL RULE

58A. Use uniform titles when:

1) you have two or more manifestations of the same work in your library *and* those manifestations have different titles

```
Dickens, Charles
  [Oliver Twist]
  The adventures of Oliver Twist
```

```
Dickens, Charles
  [Oliver Twist]
  Oliver Twist, or, The parish boy's
progress
```

2) the bibliographic resource that you are cataloguing has a title
   that is unlikely to be looked for by the users of your catalogue

```
Melville, Herman
[Moby Dick]
The whaling story from Moby Dick

Seuss, Dr.
[Grinch that stole Christmas]
Dr. Seuss's The grinch that stole
Christmas

Potter, Beatrix
[Story of Mrs. Tiggywinkle]
Die Geschichte von Frau Tiggywinkle
```

3) you are cataloguing an ancient work or a sacred scripture (see
   rule 59D)

```
Beowulf
The story of Beowulf

Talmud
New edition of the Babylonian Talmud
```

4) you are cataloguing a collection of, or selections from, the
   works of a person (see rule 60).

58B. Do not use uniform titles for revisions of works, even when those
revisions have different titles.

```
Wodehouse, P.G.
Three men and a maid

Wodehouse, P.G.
The girl on the boat
```
   (a revised edition of Three men and a maid)

59. INDIVIDUAL TITLES

59A. If you use a uniform title, choose the title by which the work is
best known. Decide this by consulting reference sources (including

other catalogues) *and* other manifestations of the same work. If you are in doubt as to which title is the best known, use the earliest title.

59B. Choose a title in the original language, unless you are cataloguing an older work originally written in a nonroman alphabet language (see rule 59C).

```
Dickens, Charles
  [Martin Chuzzlewit]
  The life and adventures of Martin
Chuzzlewit

Swift, Jonathan
  [Gulliver's travels]
  The travels of Lemuel Gulliver

Mozart, Wolfgang Amadeus
  [Don Giovanni]
  Il dissoluto punito

Hemingway, Ernest
  [Sun also rises]
  Fiesta

Wodehouse, P.G.
  [Right ho, Jeeves]
  Brinkley Manor
```
       (Brinkley Manor *is the American title of the earlier British publication* Right ho, Jeeves)
```
Malory, Thomas
  [Morte d'Arthur]
  King Arthur and the knights of the
Round Table

Caesar, Julius
  [De bello Gallico]
  Caesar's Gallic wars
```

59C. If an older work was originally in a language not written in the roman alphabet (Russian, Greek, Arabic, etc.), choose the title by which the work is best known in English-language reference sources.

```
Arabian nights
  The book of 1001 nights

Homer
  [Iliad]
  The sacking of Troy

Aristophanes
  [Frogs]
  A literal translation of
Aristophanes' The frogs
```

59D. Sacred scriptures

Use the uniform title "Bible" for the Bible.

```
Bible
  The Holy Bible
```

In cataloguing a part of the Bible, add "N.T." or "O.T." and, if appropriate, the name of the part.

```
Bible. N.T.
  The New Testament of Our Lord and
Saviour Jesus Christ

Bible. N.T. Gospels
  The Gospels of Matthew, Mark, Luke,
and John

Bible. O.T. Genesis
  The book of Genesis
```

For sacred scriptures other than the Bible, use the form of title found in English-language reference sources.

```
Talmud

Avesta

Book of Mormon
```

60. COLLECTIVE TITLES

60A. Complete works

Use the uniform title "Works" for the complete works of a person.

```
Shakespeare, William
  [Works]
  The complete works of Shakespeare

Shakespeare, William
  [Works]
  Shakespeare's works
```

60B. Selections

Use the uniform title "Selections" for selected works, or extracts from works, in more than one form by the same person.

```
Burns, Robert
  [Selections]
  Poems and letters of Robert Burns
```

60C. Works in one form

Use an appropriate uniform title in English for a collection of all the works in one form by one person.

```
Scott, Walter
  [Novels]
  The Waverley novels

Beethoven, Ludwig van
  [Symphonies]
  Beethoven's symphonies
```

61. ADDED ENTRIES AND REFERENCES

61A. Works entered under uniform title

Make an added entry (see rule 29B5) under the title proper of each bibliographic resource entered under a uniform title.

```
Arabian nights
   The thousand and one nights
```
Added entry under: Thousand and one nights

61B. Works entered under a name heading

Make a reference from the name heading and the title proper, *and* make an added entry under the title proper, of each bibliographic resource entered under a name heading and a uniform title.

```
United States
   [Constitution]
   Your rugged Constitution
```
Reference from: United States. Your rugged Constitution
Added entry under: Your rugged Constitution

```
Twain, Mark
   [Tom Sawyer]
   The adventures of Tom Sawyer
```
Reference from: Twain, Mark. Adventures of Tom Sawyer
Added entry under: Adventures of Tom Sawyer

```
Scott, Walter
   [Novels]
   The Waverley novels
```
Reference from: Scott, Walter. Waverley novels
Added entry under: Waverley novels

References

Contents

62. GENERAL RULE

62A. "See" references

Apply this rule to a person *or* corporate body *or* work when he, she, or it is known by a name *or* form of name *or* title that differs from the one used as the heading for that person *or* body *or* as the uniform title for that work.

Make a "see" reference from the variant form to the one used. Do not make a reference, however, if that reference would file in your catalogue so close to the heading as to be unnecessary.

Make additions to variant names as necessary (see rules 40–43, 51, and 52C).

62B. "See also" references

If two headings or titles are closely related, make "see also" references to connect them (see rules 63B, 64B, and 65B).

63. NAMES OF PERSONS

63A. "See" references

63A1. Refer from a name *or* form of name used by a person *or* found in reference sources, if it differs significantly from that used in the heading for that person.

Typical instances are:

Pseudonym to real name

> Yellowplush, Mr.
> see Thackeray, William

> Titmarsh, Michael Angelo
> see Thackeray, William

Real name to pseudonym

> Montgomery, Bruce
> see Crispin, Edmund

> Munro, Hector Hugh
> see Saki

Secular name to name in religion

> Kiernan, Bridget
> see De Lourdes, Sister

Earlier name to later name

> Barrett, Elizabeth
> see Browning, Elizabeth Barrett

> Spencer, Diana
> see Diana, Princess of Wales

> Bouvier, Jacqueline
> see Onassis, Jacqueline

> Kennedy, Jacqueline
> see Onassis, Jacqueline

Fuller name to briefer name

```
Mozart, Johann Chrysostom Wolfgang
  Amadeus
  see Mozart, Wolfgang Amadeus

Davies, William Henry
  see Davies, W.H. (William Henry)

Ciccone, Madonna Louise
  see Madonna (Singer/actress)

Doolittle, Hilda
  see H.D.
```

Briefer name to fuller name

```
Embleton, G.A.
  see Embleton, Gerry
```

63A2. Refer from elements of a name other than the entry element (see rules 33–39) if a person might be sought under that other element. Typical instances are:

Different elements of a compound name

```
West, Vita Sackville-
  see Sackville-West, Vita
```

Part of surname following a prefix

```
Maurier, Daphne du
  see Du Maurier, Daphne
```

Prefix

```
De Graffigny, Françoise
  see Graffigny, Françoise de
```

Part of a name not containing a surname

```
Gopal, Ram
  see Ram Gopal

Muhammad Ali
  see Ali, Muhammad
```

Inverted form of name consisting of initials

```
A., N.J.
    see N.J.A.
```

Direct form of name

```
Dr. Seuss
    see Seuss, Dr.
```

63B. "See also" references

If the same person is entered under two or more headings, make "see also" references to connect those headings.

```
Stewart, J.I.M.
    see also Innes, Michael

Innes, Michael
    see also Stewart, J.I.M.

Hibbert, Eleanor
    see also
    Carr, Philippa
    Holt, Victoria
    Kellow, Kathleen
    Plaidy, Jean
        (make similar references under each of the other
        headings)
```

64. NAMES OF CORPORATE BODIES

64A. "See" references

64A1. Refer from a name *or* form of name used by a body *or* found in reference sources if it differs from that used in the heading for the body.
   Typical instances are:

Different name

```
Common Market
    see European Union
```

European Community
　　see European Union

Quakers
　　see Society of Friends

United States. State Department
　　see United States. Department of
　　　State

Different language

Croix rouge
　　see Red Cross

Briefer form

H.M.S.O.
　　see Her Majesty's Stationery Office

American Red Cross
　　see American National Red Cross

Gestapo
　　see Germany. Geheime Staatspolizei

Fuller form

International Business Machines
　　see IBM

Religious Society of Friends
　　see Society of Friends

European Atomic Community
　　see Euratom

Different spelling

Rumania
　　see Romania

Inverted form of name

Woolworth (F.W.) Company
　　see F.W. Woolworth Company

```
Madden (Henry) Library
    see Henry Madden Library
```

Initials to acronym

```
U.N.E.S.C.O.
    see Unesco
```

64A2. Refer to a name entered directly from the name as a subordinate entry.

```
California State University, Fresno.
    Henry Madden Library
    see Henry Madden Library

American Library Association. Library
    and Information Technology
    Association
    see Library and Information
        Technology Association

United States. Amtrak
    see Amtrak

United States. Tennessee Valley
    Authority
    see Tennessee Valley Authority
```

64B. "See also" references

Make "see also" references between independently entered but related corporate bodies. If necessary, explain the relationship in the reference.

```
Freemasons
    see also
    Royal and Select Masters
    Scottish Rite (Masonic order)
        (make similar references under each of the other
        headings)

Radio Writers Guild
    see also the later heading:
    Writers Guild of America, West
```

```
Screen Writers' Guild
  see also the later heading:
  Writers Guild of America, West

Writers Guild of America, West
  see also the earlier headings:
  Radio Writers Guild
  Screen Writers' Guild

England
  see also (for 1536-1706)
  England and Wales
  and (for 1707 to 1800)
  Great Britain
  and (for 1801 to date)
  United Kingdom
```
  (make similar references under each of the other headings)

65. TITLES

65A. "See" references

65A1. Make a "see" reference from the name heading and the title proper of each item to the name heading and the uniform title of the work (see also rule 61).

```
Dickens, Charles
  The ersonal history of David
Copperfield
  see Dickens, Charles
        David Copperfield
```

65A2. Make a "see" reference from variants of the title (other than titles proper of items being catalogued, see rule 61) to the uniform title *or* name heading and uniform title.

```
Thousand and one nights
  see Arabian nights
```

```
Carroll, Lewis
   Alice's adventures in Wonderland
   see Carroll, Lewis
         Alice in Wonderland
```

65A3. Make a "see" reference from the name heading (where applicable) and collective title of a work, the parts of which are catalogued separately, to the heading and title *or* title of each part.

```
Tolkien, J.R.R.
   Lord of the rings. 2, Two towers
   see Tolkien, J.R.R.
         Two towers

Arabian nights. Sindbad the sailor
   see Sindbad the sailor
```

65A4. Make a "see" reference from the title of a part of a work to the heading and/or title of the work catalogued as a whole.

```
Old Testament
   see Bible. O.T.

Pentateuch
   see
   Bible. O.T. Pentateuch
   Bible. O.T. Genesis
   [etc.]
```

65B. "See also" references

Make "see also" references to connect related works (see rule 28).

```
Kerr, Orpheus C.
   The cloven foot
   see also Dickens, Charles
               Edwin Drood
   (the Kerr work is an adaptation of Edwin Drood)
   Added entry under Dickens (see rule 28) makes "see also"
   reference from Dickens unnecessary
```

Bart, Lionel
    Oliver!
    <u>see also</u> Dickens, Charles
                Oliver Twist
    (*the Bart work is based on the novel by Dickens*)
Added entry under Dickens (see rule 28) makes "see also"
    reference from Dickens unnecessary

Capitalization

a. HEADINGS

a1. General rule

Capitalize personal and corporate names used as headings and corporate names used as subheadings in accordance with normal usage in the language. For example, capitalize all nouns, adjectives, and verbs in English names. Always capitalize the first word in a name.

```
John, the Baptist

H.D.

De la Mare, Walter

Beauvoir, Simone de

Physician

Third Order Regular of St. Francis

Société de chimie physique

Ontario. High Court of Justice
```

a2. Additions to headings for persons

Capitalize additions to headings for persons (see rules 40–42) in accordance with normal usage in the language. If the addition is given in parentheses, capitalize the first word of the addition and any proper noun or adjective.

```
Moses, Grandma

Deidier, abbé

Emma, of Rheims
```

```
Taj Mahal (Musician)

Smith, Joan E. (Joan Eleanor)
```

a3. Additions to names of corporate bodies

Capitalize the first word of each addition to the name of a corporate body.

```
Bounty (Ship)

Knights Templar (Masonic order)

Nine Inch Nails (Rock group)

Middlesex (England : County)
```

b. TITLE AND STATEMENT OF RESPONSIBILITY AREA

b1. Title elements (general rule)

Capitalize the first word of a title proper, an alternative title, or a parallel title (including quoted titles). Capitalize other words, including the first word of any other title information element, in accordance with normal usage in the language. In English, capitalize only proper nouns and proper adjectives.

```
The perils of Pauline

The 1919/20 Breasted Expedition to the
Near East

Les enfants du paradis

IV informe de gobierno

Shakespeare's The two gentlemen of
Verona

Time out of mind

Journal of bat studies

Introduction to the World Wide Web
```

Still life with bottle and grapes

The Edinburgh world atlas, or, Advanced atlas of modern geography

Strassenkarte der Schweiz = Road map of Switzerland

The greenwood tree : newsletter of the Somerset and Dorset Family History Society

Quo vadis? : a narrative from the time of Nero

King Henry the Eighth ; and, The tempest

An interpretation of The ring and the book

Selections from Idylls of the king

Supplement to The Oxford companion to Canadian history and literature

b2. Titles preceded by dashes

Do not capitalize the first word of a title if it is preceded by a dash indicating that the beginning of the phrase from which the title was derived has been omitted.

-- loved I not honour more

b3. Grammatically independent titles of supplements and sections

If the title proper of a supplement or section consists of two or more parts not linked grammatically, capitalize the first word of the title of the second and any subsequent part.

The Travelling Wilburys. Part one

Ecology. Student handbook

Journal of biosocial science. Supplement

Progress in nuclear energy. Series 2, Reactors

Glossary

This glossary contains definitions of some of the more important cataloguing terms used in these rules. The terms have been defined only within the context of the rules. For definitions of other terms, consult the full *AACR2, or* standard glossaries of bibliographic and library terms, *or* technical dictionaries.

Access point. A name, title, word, or phrase under which a bibliographic record may be searched and identified. *Also known as* Heading.

Accompanying material. Material issued with, and intended to be used with, the bibliographic resource being catalogued.

Activity card. A card printed with words, numbers, and/or pictures used as the basis for a specific learning activity. Usually issued in sets. *See also* Game, Kit.

Added entry. An entry, other than the main entry, by which a bibliographic resource is represented in a catalogue. *See also* Main entry.

Alternative title. The second part of a title proper that consists of two parts joined by the word *or* or its equivalent in another language (for example, *Crushed violet, or, A servant girl's tale*).

Analytical entry. An entry for a part of a bibliographic resource for the whole of which an entry has also been made.

Anonymous. Of unknown authorship.

Area. A major section of the bibliographic description (see rule 0C). *See also* Element.

Art original. An original work of art.

Art print. An engraving, etc., printed from the plate prepared by the artist.

Art reproduction. A mechanical, photographic, or computer-produced copy of a work of art, generally as part of a commercial edition.

Atlas. A volume of maps, plates, engravings, tables, etc., with or without descriptive text. An atlas may be an independent publication, or it may have been issued to accompany one or more volumes of text.

Author. The person chiefly responsible for the intellectual or artistic content of a work.

Author/title added entry. See Name/title added entry.

Author/title reference. See Name/title reference.

Bibliographic resource. A manifestation of a work that forms the basis for bibliographic description. Sometimes referred to as an "item," a bibliographic resource could be a book or other printed document, an electronic resource, a graphic such as a poster or art work, a video or film, a sound recording, or any other means by which recorded knowledge and information are communicated.

Cartographic material. Any material representing the whole or part of the Earth or any other celestial body. A map, globe, atlas, cartographic chart, etc.

Catalogue. A list of library materials contained in part of a library's collection, a whole library collection, or the collections of a group of libraries, arranged according to some definite plan.

Chart. An opaque sheet containing graphic or tabular data (for example, a wall chart).

Chart (cartographic). A map designed for navigation.

Chief source of information. The source in a bibliographic resource preferred as the source from which data given in the bibliographic description are taken.

Collaborator. A person who works with one or more associates to produce a work. For collaborators who make the same kind of contribution, see rule 25. For collaborators who make different kinds of contribution, as in the case of collaboration between an artist and a writer, see rule 27. *See also* Joint author, Mixed responsibility, Shared responsibility.

Collective title. A title proper for a bibliographic resource containing two or more works.

Coloured illustration. An illustration in two or more colours.

Compiler. A person who produces a collection by putting together material from the works of two or more persons or bodies. *See also* Editor.

Compound surname. A surname consisting of two or more proper names, sometimes connected by a hyphen.

Computer file. See Electronic resource.

Conference. 1. A meeting for the purpose of discussing and/or acting upon a topic. 2. A legislative or governing meeting of the representatives of a corporate body.

Container. A box, record sleeve, folder, etc., in which a bibliographic resource is issued.

Corporate body. An organization or group of persons that is identified by a particular name (for example, an association, government, government agency, religious body, local church, conference).

Cross-reference. See Reference.

Diorama. A three-dimensional representation of a scene created by placing objects, figures, etc., in front of a two-dimensional background.

Distributor. An agent or agency (other than a publisher) that markets an item.

Edition: Books, etc. All copies of a printed resource produced from essentially the same type image and issued by the same entity.

Edition: Other materials. All copies of a bibliographic resource containing essentially the same content and issued by the same entity.

Edition: Unpublished items. All copies made from the same production (for example, the original and carbon copies of a typescript; the copies of a homemade videotape).

Editor. A person who prepares other people's work for publication. *See also* Compiler.

Electronic resource. Material (data and/or program(s)) encoded for manipulation by a computer. This material may require the use of a peripheral directly connected to a computer (e.g., CD-ROM drive) or a connection to a computer network (e.g., the Internet).

Element. A word, phrase, or group of characters representing a distinct unit of bibliographic information and forming part of an area of the description. *See also* Area.

Entry. A record of a bibliographic resource in a catalogue. *See also* Heading.

Filing title. See Uniform title.

Filmstrip. A length of film containing a succession of images intended for projection one at a time.

Flash card. A card or other opaque material printed with words, numerals, or pictures and designed for rapid display.

Game. A set of materials designed for play according to rules. *See also* Activity card, Kit.

General material designation. A term indicating the broad class of material to which a bibliographic resource belongs (for example, "sound recording," "electronic resource"). *See also* Specific material designation.

Globe. A model of the Earth or another celestial body depicted on the surface of a sphere.

Heading. A name, word, or phrase placed at the head of a catalogue entry to provide an access point. *Also known as* Access point.

Impression. All copies of an edition of a book or other printed material printed at one time. *See also* Reprint.

Integrating resource. A bibliographic resource that is added to or changed by updates that are integrated into the whole. Loose-leaf publications and Websites are examples of integrating resources. *See also* Serial.

International Standard Book Number (ISBN). See Standard number.

International Standard Serial Number (ISSN). See Standard number.

Item. See Bibliographic resource.

Joint author. A person with shared responsibility for a work. *See also* Shared responsibility.

Kit. 1. A bibliographic resource containing two or more categories of material, no one of which is identifiable as being predominant; also called "multimedia item." 2. A bibliographic resource consisting of a package of textual materials (for example, a "lab kit"). *See also* Activity card, Game.

Main entry. A catalogue entry for which the access point is the main entry heading (see rules 21–28). *See also* Added entry.

Manuscript. A text, musical score, map, etc., that is inscribed, hand-written, typewritten, or, in some cases, printed from a computer.

Masthead. The statement of title, ownership, editors, etc., of a newspaper or periodical. In the case of newspapers it is often found on the editorial page or at the top of page 1. In the case of periodicals, it is often found on the contents page.

Microform. Any medium, transparent or opaque, bearing microimages. Microforms include microfilms, microfiches, micro-opaques, etc.

Microscope slide. A slide holding a minute object to be viewed through a microscope or by a microprojector.

Mixed authorship. See Mixed responsibility.

Mixed responsibility. A work of mixed responsibility is one in which different persons or bodies contribute to the intellectual or artistic content by performing different kinds of activities (for example, adapting or illustrating a work written by another person). *See also* Shared responsibility.

Model. A three-dimensional representation.

Monograph. A bibliographic resource that is (1) complete (in one or more parts), or (2) intended to be completed in a stated number of separate parts.

Multimedia item. 1. A kit. *See* Kit, first definition. 2. A bibliographic resource made up of two or more media of communication (e.g., a textual, video, and sound electronic resource).

Multipart item. A monograph consisting of two or more physical pieces. *See also* Monograph.

Name/title added entry. An added entry with an access point consisting of the name of a person or corporate body and a title.

Name/title reference. A reference in which one or both parts consist of the name of a person or a corporate body and a title.

Numbering. The identification of each of the successive items of a bibliographic resource. It can include a numeral, a letter, any other character, or the combination of these with or without an accompanying word (volume, number, etc.) and/or a chronological designation.

Other title information. Any title borne by a bibliographic resource other than the title proper, alternative title, or parallel title (for example, a subtitle). Other title information does not include variations on the title (for example, spine titles, sleeve titles).

Parallel title. The title proper in another language and/or script.

Part. One of the units into which a bibliographic resource has been divided by the author, publisher, or manufacturer.

Personal author. See Author.

Picture. A two-dimensional visual representation accessible to the naked eye. Use as a specific material designation (see rule 5B) when a more specific term (for example, "art original," "photograph") is not appropriate.

Predominant name: Corporate bodies. The name or form of name of a body that appears most frequently in (1) bibliographic resources that are issued by the body or with which the body is connected *or* (2) reference sources. Prefer the name or form of name that appears in the first to those in the second.

Predominant name: Persons. The name or form of name of a person that appears most frequently in (1) bibliographic resources that are manifestations of the person's works or to which the person has contributed *or* (2) reference sources. Prefer the name or form of name that appears in the first to those in the second.

Pseudonym. A name assumed by an author.

Realia. The general material designation (see rule 1C) for actual objects (artefacts or specimens) as opposed to replicas.

Reference. 1. A "See" reference is a direction from one form of a name or title to another. 2. A "See also" reference is a direction from one access point to another. *See also* Name/title reference.

Reference sources. Publications (not just reference works) from which authoritative information may be obtained.

Related body. A corporate body that has a relation to another body other than that of subordination. Related bodies include those that are founded but not controlled by other bodies; those that provide financial and/or other types of assistance to other bodies, such as "friends" groups; those whose members are also members of other bodies, such as employees' associations and alumni associations.

Reprint. 1. A new printing of a book or other printed material made from the original type image. 2. A new issue of a book or other printed material with substantially unchanged text.

Romanization. Conversion of words not written in the roman alphabet to roman-alphabet form.

Section (serials). A separately published part of a serial with its own designation.

Serial. A bibliographic resource in any format that is issued in successive parts (usually bearing numerical or chronological designations) *and* intended to be continued indefinitely. Examples are periodicals; electronic journals; newspapers; annuals (reports, yearbooks, etc.); the journals, memoirs, proceedings, transactions, etc., of societies; and monographic series. *See also* Integrating resource.

Series. A group of separate bibliographic resources related to one another by the fact that each bears, in addition to its own title proper, a collective title applying to the group as a whole.

Shared responsibility. Collaboration between two or more persons or bodies performing the same kind of activity in the creation of the intellectual or artistic content of a work. *See also* Collaborator, Joint author.

Slide. Transparent material, usually held in a mount, on which there is a two-dimensional image and that is designed for use in a projector or viewer.

Specific material designation. A term indicating the special class of material to which a bibliographic resource belongs (for example, "sound disc," "computer optical disc"). *See also* General material designation.

Spine title. The title that appears on the spine of a book.

Standard number. The International Standard Number (ISN) (for example, International Standard Book Number or ISBN, International Standard Serial Number or ISSN, or any other internationally agreed upon number that identifies a bibliographic resource uniquely).

Statement of responsibility. A statement, transcribed from the item being described, relating to authors *or* to corporate bodies issuing the bibliographic resource *or* to persons or corporate bodies responsible for the performance of the content of the bibliographic resource.

Subordinate body. A corporate body that is an administrative part of a larger body.

Subseries. A series within a series.

Subtitle. See Other title information.

Supplement. A separately issued bibliographic resource that brings up-to-date or otherwise continues an already published bibliographic resource.

Supplied title. The title provided by the cataloguer for a bibliographic resource that lacks a title proper.

Surname. A family name or name used as a family name.

Technical drawing. A drawing made for use in a technical context (for example, engineering).

Title. A word, phrase, character, or group of characters naming a bibliographic resource or the work of which it is a manifestation.

Title page. A page at or near the beginning of a book, atlas, musical score, etc., bearing the title proper. The title page does not include the page on the back of the title leaf (sometimes called the title page verso).

Title proper. The chief name of a bibliographic resource, including any alternative title but excluding parallel titles and other title information.

Title screen. The first or one of the first screens seen when using an electronic resource. It bears the fullest statement of the title of the resource and may bear statements of responsibility, etc.

Toy. An object designed for imaginative play or amusement.

Transparency. A sheet of transparent material bearing an image and designed for use with an overhead projector or a light box. It may be mounted in a frame.

Uniform title. 1. The title by which a work that has appeared under varying titles is to be identified for cataloguing purposes. 2. A conventional collective title (for example, "Works").

Comparative Table
of Rule Numbers

This table lists the rules in *AACR2* that correspond, or correspond most nearly, to the rules in the *Concise AACR2*. In Part 1, also consult any correspondingly numbered rules in *AACR2* chapters 2–12 if you need detailed guidance. For example, if the reference is to *AACR2* rule 1.1A1, you may wish to consult 2.1A1, 3.1A1, etc.

Concise AACR2 PART 1	AACR2 PART 1	Concise AACR2 PART 1	AACR2 PART 1
0A	1.0A1, 1.0A2, 1.1A2, and .0B rules in chapters 2–12	4D	1.4D
		4E	1.4F
		5	1.5
		5A1	1.5A1
0B	1.0A3	5B	1.5B
0C	1.0B	5B2	2.5B1–2.5B15
0D	1.0C	5B3	2.5B16–2.5B21
0E	1.0D	5B4	1.5B5
1	1.1	5C	1.5C
1A1	1.1A1	5D	1.5D
1B	1.1B	5E	1.5E
1C	1.1C	6	1.6
1D	1.1D	6A1	1.6A1
1E	1.1E	6B	1.6B
1F	1.1F	6C	1.6E
1G	1.1G	6D	1.6G
2	1.2	6E	1.6H
2A1	1.2A1	6F	1.6J
2B	1.2B	7	1.7
2C	1.2C	7A2	1.7A1
3	1.3	7A3	1.7A2
3A	12.3	7A4	1.7A3
3B	3.3	7B1	12.7B1 and 9.7B1
3C	5.3	7B2	1.7B1
4	1.4	7B3	1.7B2
4A1	1.4A1	7B4	1.7B2
4B	1.4B	7B5	1.7B3–1.7B5, and 9.7B3
4C	1.4C		

Concise AACR2 PART 1	AACR2 PART I
7B6	1.7B6
7B7	1.7B7
7B8	1.7B9
7B9	1.7B10
7B10	1.7B11
7B11	1.7B14
7B12	1.7B16
7B13	1.7B17
7B14	1.7B18
7B15	1.7B20
7B16	1.7B21
8	1.8
8A	1.8A
8B	1.8B
9	1.9
10	1.10
11	1.11

Concise AACR2 PART 2	AACR2 PART II
21A	21.0A
21B	21.0B
21C	21.0C
22	21.2
22A	21.2C2
22B	21.2A
22C	21.2C
22D	21.2B
23A	21.1A
23B	21.1B
23C	21.1C
24A	21.4A
24B	21.4B
25A	21.6A
25B	21.6B
25C	21.6C
26A	21.7A
26B	21.7B
26C	21.7C
27A	21.8
27B	21.9–21.23

Concise AACR2 PART 2	AACR2 PART II
27C	21.24–21.27
28	21.28
29A	21.29
29B1	21.30A
29B2	21.30B–21.30E
29B3	21.30F
29B4	21.30G
29B5	21.30J
29B6	21.30K
29B7	21.30L
29B8	21.30M and 13.1–13.6
31	22.1
32A	22.2B and 21.6D
32B	22.2A and 22.2C
33	22.4A
33A	22.4B
34A	22.5A
34B	22.5B
34C	22.5C
34D	22.5D–22.5E
35	22.6
36	22.8
37	22.9A
38	22.10
39	22.11
40	22.12
41	22.11A
42	22.18
43	22.17
44	22.20
45	23.1
46	23.2 and 23.4–23.5
47	23.3
49	24.1
50A	24.3A–24.3B
50B	24.3E
50C	24.2
51A	24.4A
51B	24.4C2
51C	24.4C1 and 24.4C3–24.4C7

Concise AACR2 PART 2	*AACR2* PART II	*Concise AACR2* PART 2	*AACR2* PART II
52A	24.3F	59B	25.3
52B	24.7A	59C	25.4
52C	24.7B	59D	25.17–25.18
52D	24.7B4	60A	25.8
53	24.12	60B	25.9
54	24.13	60C	25.10
55A	24.18	61	25.2E and 26.4
55B	24.20	62	26.1
56A	24.14 and 24.19	63	26.2
56B	24.24	64	26.3
57	25.1	65	26.4
57B	25.2A	Appendix I	Appendix A
57C	25.2C	Appendix II	Appendix D
58	25.1A		

Index

The index covers the Introduction, rules, and Appendices, but not examples or works cited in any of the rules or appendices. Index entries beginning "Introduction" refer to page numbers. Index entries beginning with numerals refer to rule numbers. Index entries beginning App. refer to the appendices. Footnotes are indicated by *n* after the rule number.

The index is alphabetized word by word, disregarding punctuation.

Numbers
   in edition statement, 2B
   in headings for conferences, 52C,
      52D
Numerals as personal names, 38

O

Objects, *see* Realia
Office, title of, *see* Titles of position or
   office
Old Testament, uniform titles, 59D
Omissions
   from names of conferences, 52B
   other title information, 1E3
   from statements of responsibility,
      1F5–1F7
OPACs
   display of records in, Introduction
      p. 3
   punctuation in, 0D
Optical discs
   diameter, 5D(8)
   extent, 5B1(c), 5B1(l)
optional rules in AACR2, Introduction
   p. 3, 6
Originals, notes on, 11
Other title information
   definition, App. II
   general rule, 1E

P

Pagination, *see* Extent of resource
Pamphlets, *see* Books
Parallel titles, 1D
   capitalization, App. I b1
   definition, App. II
Paraphrases, *see* Adaptations
Part (music), extent, 5B1(h)
Particles, names with, *see* Prefixes, surnames with
Parts of works
   definition, App. II
   references, 65A3
   title proper for, 1B4

Performers and performance groups
   added entries, 29B2(d)
   entries for, 23B2(f), 24B
   of musical works by one person,
      27B2(a)
   of works by many persons, 27B1(g)
Periodicals, *see* Serials
Personal authors, entry, 23A, *see also*
   Authors and authorship; Personal
   names, headings
   definition, 23A1
   works by a single person, 24A
   works by two or more persons,
      23A2
Personal names, headings, 30–43, *see
   also* Compound surnames;
   Forenames (given names);
   Pseudonyms; Surnames
   capitalization, App. I a1, App. I a2
   choice of, 30
   different names or forms of the
      same name, 32B
   entry element, 33
   identical names, distinguishing,
      42–44
   initials, expansion of, 42
   initials, letters, or numerals as, 38
   order of elements, 33A
   in other languages, see *specific
      language*
   pseudonyms, 32A
   references, 63
   surname, entry under, 34
   titles of nobility, 35
   words or phrases as names, 31D
Photocopies, *see* Reproductions
Phrases, *see* Words or phrases
Physical description area, 5
   multimedia resources, 10C2
   notes on, 7B9
Pictures
   definition, App. II
   extent, 5B1(a)
   general material designation, 1C1
Place names, *see* Geographic names
Place of conferences, 52C, 52D

U

LaVergne, TN USA
08 September 2010
196318LV00005B/1/P